Show us y...

–Every great team is built around a strong spine, so they say. The MOTD
line-up is no different: there's Hansen and Lawrenson giving absolutely
away at the back, Brooking providing some incisive input in the middle,
lad Lineker up front, presenting the football show that always hits the target. But football is played on grass,
not in a TV studio, we hear you cry. Fair enough – let's take a look at the playing careers of our pundits. Come
on, you four - put up or shut up, and... **SHOW US YOUR MEDALS!**

GARY LINEKER

Born: 30 / 11 / 60
Birthplace: Leicester

Clubs Played For:

LEICESTER CITY	
EVERTON	
BARCELONA	
TOTTENHAM HOTSPUR	
NAGOYA GRAMPUS EIGHT (of Japan)	

International Caps For England: 80
International Goals: 48

 ONE of the greatest goalscorers to grace the game, Gary's total for England is only one short of the record held by Sir Bobby Charlton. He won the coveted Golden Boot as the top scorer in the 1986 World Cup, and – almost uniquely in the modern game – he was never booked or sent off. His honours' haul includes Spanish Cup and European Cup Winners' Cup successes at Barcelona, and an FA Cup winner's medal at Tottenham. In his one season for Everton, he totalled 38 goals from 52 appearances when the Merseyside club so very nearly claimed the 'double'. The same season he was voted both PFA and Football Writers' Association Player of the Year. With more than 200 League goals both here and abroad to his name, Gary's game was based on lightning pace, and on a willingness to make countless runs in the box in anticipation of crosses reaching him. Nine times out of ten, the ball never arrived, but on that tenth occasion, Gary was there to apply the deadly striker's finish.

ALAN HANSEN

Born: 13 / 6 / 55
Birthplace: ALLOA
Clubs Played For:

PARTICK THISTLE	
LIVERPOOL	

International Caps For Scotland: 26

 THERE are Liverpool fans who blame their team's relatively poor record in the 1990s on Alan Hansen.
That's because he was simply too good – since injury forced him to give up playing at the start

£5.99

of that decade, he has proven to be utterly irreplaceable. For thirteen years he was a colossus at centre-back, exuding calm control by being able to read the game so well. Easily the classiest defender Scotland has ever produced – and many judges regard it as a scandal that he didn't play more times for his country – he always looked to have time when in possession. Few in the game, if any, have looked better when carrying the ball forward out of defence to instigate attacks. Alan skippered Liverpool to the 'double' in 1986, while a glance at his astonishing winner's medal collection – 3 European Cups, 8 League Championships, 2 FA Cups, 3 League Cups – tells you everything you need to know.

TREVOR BROOKING

Born: 2 / 10 / 48
Birthplace: BARKING
Club Played For:

WEST HAM UNITED

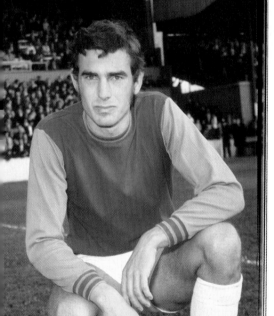

International Caps For England: 47
International Goals: 5

THERE can't be many players who have been more accurately described by their nickname than 'Clever Trevor' Brooking. A midfield playmaker of wonderful touch and guile, this one-club player was genuinely two-footed on the park. Always elegant and creative, at his peak he formed a terrific understanding with Kevin Keegan for their country. And, but for unfortunate injuries to both players, England might even have reached the Final of the 1982 World Cup. There were rumours throughout his career that a move to a 'bigger' club was on the cards for Trevor, but he stayed loyal to his beloved West Ham, making more than 600 appearances for them. He collected FA Cup winner's medals in 1975 and 1980, the latter coming when the Hammers were in the old Second Division. That Final remains the last occasion when a team from outside the top flight lifted the Cup – and our man Trevor scored the game's only goal!

MARK LAWRENSON

Born: 2 / 6 / 57
Birthplace: PRESTON

Clubs Played For:

PRESTON NORTH END

BRIGHTON & HOVE ALBION

LIVERPOOL

International Caps For Rep. Ireland: 38
International Goals: 5

POSSIBLY born with the moustache, it's as much a trademark of Mark today as superb tackles and speedy interceptions were during his playing days. In 1981, Bob Paisley paid a then record fee for Liverpool to prise defender Mark away from Brighton. Tall enough to deal with any aerial threat, athletic enough to match any striker for pace, and astute enough to time his tackling to perfection, he was everything a defender should be. Yet he was no mere stopper, possessing sufficient skills to always look confident and assured when on the ball, and – before slotting in alongside Alan Hansen at the heart of Liverpool's defence – versatile enough to play at full-back or in midfield for The Reds. He was forced out of the game through an Achilles injury, but not before he'd picked up medals for a European Cup win, 5 League titles, an FA Cup success (which completed the 'double') and 3 League Cup triumphs.

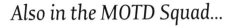
Show us your Medals

Also in the MOTD Squad...

GARTH CROOKS

MARTIN O'NEILL

MARTIN O'NEILL is almost as lively in the MOTD studios as he is on the touch-line. Never one to hold back with an opinion, the new Celtic manager's enthusiasm for the game is there for all to see. By transmitting that enthusiasm to the players he's managed, Martin steered Wycombe Wanderers from non-League football to the Second Division with successive promotions. It's also how he guided Leicester City from the First Division to the top half of the Premiership, picking up two League Cups along the way. Yet Martin could also play a bit, too – during his time at Nott'm Forest, the club won back-to-back European Cups, the League title and enjoyed two League Cup successes. He played 64 times for Northern Ireland, scoring eight times – a total just one less than the magical George Best.

GARTH CROOKS and MARK BRIGHT have enjoyed remarkably similar football lives. Both were born in Stoke, both played as strikers, both started out at local sides (Garth at Stoke City, Mark at Port Vale), both scored well over 100 League goals, and both turned out in three Wembley Finals and two further Final replays. About the only difference between them is that Mark appeared in a play-off final, plus being a winner in the Zenith Data Systems Cup competition, whilst Garth collected 2 FA Cup winner's medals.

RAY STUBBS

RAY STUBBS, meanwhile, is from the other side of the football tracks. Though good enough to have been on the books of Tranmere Rovers, Ray's talents never took him to the very top level of the game. But if Ray's football pedigree is of a humbler kind when compared to the rest of the MOTD team, he has a prize-winning edge over all of them: there is not a journalist or former-player pundit in the land who can pronounce the surname of the Birmingham City forward Peter Ndlovu quite like he can.

MARK BRIGHT

DAVID GINOLA, voted both Footballer of the Year and PFA Player of the Year in 1999, is another popular guest in the MOTD studios. The flamboyant Frenchman provides insightful views from a current top player's perspective. And two new recent signings made their debuts behind the pundits' table during Euro 2000. Leeds' boss DAVID O'LEARY – having steered his young side to a spot in the Champions League in his first full season in charge and having turned out for Arsenal a mere 722 times, collecting pairs of Championship, FA Cup and League Cup winner's medals along the way – must know something about the game! As indeed does MICK McCARTHY, who took up the unenviable challenge of filling Jack Charlton's shoes as manager of the Republic of Ireland in 1996. Only results in two sets of play-offs prevented him taking the side to France for the 1998 World Cup and to Euro 2000. A rock-solid defender in his playing days, he won the 'double' in Scotland with Celtic in 1988, the Scottish Cup again a year later, and collected 57 caps for the Republic.

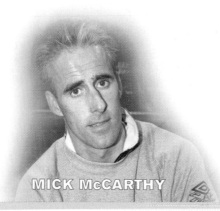

DAVID GINOLA

MICK McCARTHY

DAVID O'LEARY

Past Performers *MOTD'S Previous Front Men Who Could All Deliver*

WHILE transfers are inevitable in football, TV presenters can change sides, too. Way back in 1973, MOTD brought in a man from London Weekend Television to front the show. He stayed until the BBC temporarily lost the rights to show Football League highlights in 1989. His name - JIMMY HILL. He's not a man you can ignore, our Jim. A player with Brentford and Fulham, he was a qualified coach at the age of 24. Later, brimming with new ideas as a manager, he took then Third Division strugglers Coventry City to the old First Division in four seasons. The innovations didn't stop when he became Chairman of the club either. He brought in the country's first under-soil heating system to combat frozen pitches, and some ten years before the Taylor Report recommended the switch to all-seater stadiums, Jimmy attempted to make Highfield Road a seats-only ground. Jimmy was not to be ignored when fronting MOTD either. He doubled as both presenter and match analyst, was never shy about highlighting wrongs in the game, and often caused controversy with his opinions. Given his experience of virtually every aspect of the game, however, no-one could argue that his views lacked substance. Joining Jimmy on MOTD during that period, tackling the football news of the day, was BOB WILSON. The Arsenal goalkeeper during the side's 'double' season of 1970-71, Bob also earned full international honours with Scotland. He developed into an equally 'safe pair of hands' when presenting a variety of sports programmes for the BBC. His stint as part of the MOTD team came to an end when he moved in the opposite direction to Jimmy and joined ITV. Then, more recently, ITV signed up another former MOTD presenter when DES LYNAM made a similar transfer to Bob's. Initially, it was thought in some quarters that when the programme lost its legendary, laid-back, witty front man, MOTD would struggle to replace him. Not a bit of it ... enter Gary Lineker.

BOB WILSON

JIMMY HILL

DES LYNAM

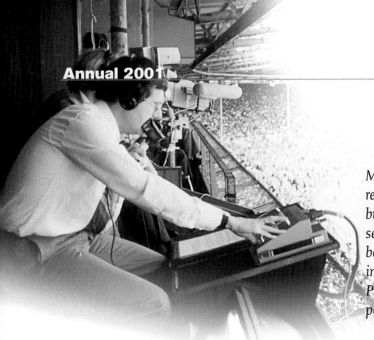

Hour by Hour
MOTD

Millions of viewers watch Match of the Day each week, relying on Britain's longest-running football programme to bring them the best of the day's soccer action from the best seat in the house. But next time those exciting pictures are beamed into your living room, stop and think about the incredible technical operation that goes into capturing Premiership highlights to form such a neat and extremely polished package

MOTD

10am

Paul McNamara   **Niall Sloane**

FOR the main game, the BBC crew arrive at the ground before most of the fans are even thinking about leaving home. But preparation will have begun long before that. The game will have been chosen by editor Niall Sloane and producer Paul McNamara three weeks in advance, and the ground will have been checked for access for all the Outside Broadcast (OB) vehicles and any platforms that might need to be built for cameras.

11am

A couple of weeks before the game, the director will have had a look to see where he wants the cameras to go. The night before the

game, the OB trucks will have rolled into the ground and all the cables run up to the camera positions, a job that takes about two and a half hours. Now the rest of the equipment is rigged up, ready for the 'look-see'.

12pm

The director sits in the Production Vehicle or 'Scanner' and talks to all his cameramen through the 'talkback'. He tells them to show him what they can see from their camera positions, so that he knows where to get the best angles during the game. Because this is one of

the day's biggest games, Football Focus will want a live interview with one of the managers, so the director has to get his commentator and interviewee to one of the pitchside

cameras to conduct the interview, which is then beamed back to Television Centre in London.

1pm

With everything up and running and first interviews safely away, everyone can go and grab some lunch. Over the years the technical staff have got to know all the best fish and chip shops and cafes around the grounds, and they head off for some vital refreshment before the match.

2pm

An hour later everyone returns to their positions for a final check of the equipment. The cameramen are all looking through the lens and the commentator is in the gantry. Everyone has headphones on. John Motson

prefers the grounds where the gantry is close to the pitch. "I like to sit further forward in the stand, with the supporters if necessary, to get more of a feel for the atmosphere," he says. Meanwhile, the programme editors and producers arrive at Television Centre in London and establish contact with the OB unit.

With about 20 minutes to go, the commentator delivers his 'Around the Grounds' report for Grandstand, with pictures shot a few minutes earlier. Barely a second of the day is wasted.

3pm

Gary Lineker and the pundits have all arrived at TV Centre to watch the matches being beamed in live. During the game they will pick out key incidents that they will want to discuss in that evening's programme and a production assistant writes down the time

and description of the incident to help the editor later on.

Over at the ground, the director watches the pictures coming in from all his cameras and chooses which shot he wants to show at any given time. He also makes sure that he records different angles of goals and other major incidents as well as shots of fans, managers, etc ('cutaways') to help the editors to join pieces of action together smoothly. All the time he keeps in contact with the cameramen and commentator to tell them what he wants to see and talk about.

When the final whistle blows the first task is to send a report in to Grandstand. Here the commentator, who has been working hard throughout the game, has to rapidly collect his thoughts and sum up the 90 minutes, including all the important details, quickly and concisely. He then has to dash off to conduct interviews with managers and players. John Motson says that one of the biggest changes he's noticed in his job has been the number of people competing with him to get post-match interviews nowadays. "The demands on the players and managers at the end of the game have increased one hundredfold."

5pm

With only one camera required for the post-match interviews, the rest of the crew can start dismantling their equipment. The cables

will be left in place until the following day because it's a three-hour job that needs daylight, but everything else will be packed away by 6pm and the OB unit can head home.

6pm

It's time for the team at TV Centre to take over. With the help of the cutaways, the action is edited down to about 20 minutes, with a couple of minutes on top for the commentator's introduction and post-match interviews. By the time the show goes live on air, all the action has been cut down into that neat, polished package ready for Gary and the team to discuss.

Not long before midnight, when the programme has finished, they have a quick chat with Niall Sloane and Paul McNamara to discuss how things went and then everybody goes their separate ways. It's the end of a very long and exhausting day.

Numbers Game

Match of the Day uses 10 cameras for the main game. This includes the wide-angle hoist camera, used for aerial shots, and a super slo-mo camera, for slow-motion action replays. Television cameras and lenses are extremely expensive. One camera plus lens can cost as much as £100,000.

Around two miles of cabling is used to connect all the cameras and microphones to the Scanner. It can be double that amount for some grounds. Great care has to be taken in

putting the cables in. It must not get in any-body's way, and when you consider how many people attend a Premiership match, that's no mean feat.

The Outside Broadcast unit usually consists of four vehicles: the Hoist; the Production Vehicle (Scanner); the Technical Support Vehicle (TSV) which carries all the cameras, microphones and other equipment; and the Cable Tender, with its great drums of cables. In addition, they take a twin generator that supplies electricity throughout and serves as back-up should the stadium's power fail.

There are about 25 technical crew plus up to 10 production personnel in the OB team, numbering 35 in total.

Cameras

The most important part of each camera is the

lens. While the hoist camera has a wide-angle lens for taking in a broad view, others have lenses that will zoom in very tight on the action. Of the 10 cameras, four will be fitted with lenses that magnify 55 times, and one will have a lens that magnifies 70 times.
Most of the action is shown from camera one, which is positioned on the main gantry, over

the half-way line – in other words, the best seat in the house. This shows the game pretty much as the commentator sees it.
Next to this is Camera Two, which also follows the action but much tighter. This is often the camera with the 70:1 lens.

Alternatively the camera at pitchside on the half-way line will have the 70:1 lens, for focusing on the faces on the bench from the far side of the pitch, for example.
Other cameras are positioned level with the edge of the penalty area, behind the goals, anywhere where the director feels he might get the most interesting shots.

Recently, MOTD added a new angle to its coverage of games - the hoist camera. This is a camera fitted with a wide-angle lens and positioned on top of a huge arm that can rise to a height of 72m. It gives an overview of the whole game, which is useful for analysis. However, if the wind is blowing at more than 25mph it is too dangerous to send up the hoist camera.

Green Screen

Unlike the old days when the studio backdrop was a piece of cardboard scenery with images on it, the graphics you now see behind Gary Lineker and the pundits aren't really there! In the studio all you will see is a plain green backdrop and the graphics are projected onto this. It's important that the presenters don't wear anything green because the projected images show up on anything of that colour. So if Gary Lineker wore a green shirt, for example, you would see it covered in MOTD graphics.

The Scanner

The Scanner, or Production Vehicle, is the heart of the whole Outside Broadcast operation. It's a 45ft truck that, from the outside, does not look big enough to house all the necessary equipment, but on the inside is like a Tardis.
On the road it measures the regulation 8ft wide, but the sides fold out to give it an extra 10ft in width in the middle section.
The Scanner is divided into four sections in all. The cab, where the driver sits, is also the Radio

Links area, from where all the signals are sent back to TV Centre.
Next comes the Vision area, where all the electronics for the cameras and microphones are housed.
Then there is the central Production area. This is where the director and engineering manager sit during the game to select and mix the visuals. There is also a production assistant who makes a note of all the important timings. In front of them is a bank of about 40 TV monitors, showing pictures from all the cameras, as well as action replays and other images. It takes great skill and concentration to make head or tail of all these images and ensure you choose the best one for each moment.

The fourth section, at the rear of the Scanner, is the Sound area. All communication between the director and his crew is sorted out from here. All the microphones feed into here and the sound is mixed for output to TV Centre.

Memories
MOTD

1964 - Match of the Day launches on BBC2 in August with Liverpool v Arsenal. The technological advance of electronic cameras and video tapes, transmitting outside broadcast events to a central location for editing, makes the whole thing possible, No longer does film footage have to be physically removed from a camera. Yet the programme starts as a nervous experiment rather than a market leader. The first broadcast attracts a television audience of just 20,000.

Jimmy smiles amongst a see of faces

Presenters Parry, Motson & Gubba

1966 - England's World Cup triumph propels the show into a BBC1 Saturday evening slot. Its audience is growing and growing.

1971 - The invention of the 'video disc', allowing slo-mo replays, giving birth to 'trial by television'.

1972 - Hereford beat Newcastle 2-1 in the FA Cup and a new commentator, John Motson, completes his

first dramatic game. By now, the MOTD viewing figures have reached a massive 12 million.

1973 - The man known as 'The Chin', Jimmy Hill, signs from ITV to front the programme with retired Arsenal goalie Bob Wilson.

1980 - After 16 seasons in its Saturday night slot, Match of the Day moves to Sunday afternoons. Jimmy and Bob swap suits for shirtsleeves and pullovers.

1980 - MOTD cameras capture Clive Allen's shot for Crystal Palace against Coventry hitting the stanchion inside the goal and bouncing straight back out. Both ref and linesman assume it has hit the bar and disallow the goal. Most clubs redesign their netting as a result – a move instigated by the Coventry chairman – none other than presenter Jimmy Hill!

1981 - The return of Match of the Day to the Saturday evening slot kicks-off with Swansea's stirring 5-1 win over Leeds.

1982 - The programme goes out again on Sunday afternoon, yet another twist in the ongoing saga of the BBC's turn and turnabout arrangement with ITV.

1983 - Live League football comes to the nation's screens as the BBC and ITV sign a deal with the Football League for seven games each to be transmitted per season.

1985 - Match of the Day's 21st anniversary celebrations are curtailed by the disasters of the Bradford fire and the crowd deaths at Heysel.

1988 - ITV secure rights to League football for four years. The BBC counter with a five-year FA Cup deal and rename the programme Match of the Day – the Road to Wembley.

1989 - The programme's silver jubilee is overshadowed by the disaster at Hillsborough.

1992 - The BBC enters into a partnership with Sky Sports to cover highlights of the new Premier League. The old Match of the Day formula is revived, but now included are all of the goals from the other games in the Premiership that day.

Alan Parry

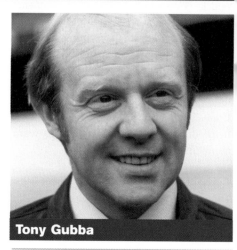

Tony Gubba

1999 - Gary Lineker moves into the hot-seat as Des Lynam is transferred to the other channel. Ex-pro players are now seated around the famous MOTD desk, notably Alan Hansen, Trevor Brooking and Mark Lawrenson. New gadgetry means that goals can be analysed better, including scoring distances and speed of shots at goal.

2000 - The BBC pledges its commitment to the excellent standards it has achieved in football.

Old and new

*Season in, season out, football's conveyor belt of talent thankfully turns out its continuous crop of gifted youngsters – and who better to judge the best of the new kids than TREVOR BROOKING, as he presents his ...***Top 30 Under 20**

Jeremie Aliadiere

Was signed by Arsenal from the French FA's School of Excellence in January 1999 for £1.3m, even though he'll only turn 18 in March 2001. Arsenal's French scout Damian Angier-Cornelli recommended the forward to Arséne Wenger, who decided to sign him after watching him in an U-15 international. The director of the French School of Excellence, Claude Dosset, describes him as the new van Basten, and Wenger reputedly sees him as a likely first-teamer by 2002.

Moritz Volz

Left Gelsenkirchen club Schalke 04 for Arsenal in the summer of 1999. Has captained the German U-15 side, and at international level plays either at right-back or on the right of three centre-backs. Hopes to develop into a midfielder in England so he can develop the passing side of his game. Is reported to be earning £150,000 a year at Highbury, despite not being 18 until January 2001.

Mikael Forssell

Chelsea forward who will only turn 20 in March 2001. He emerged as a 16-year-old playing for the Finnish champions HJK Helsinki. Chelsea signed him one year later and he immediately repaid them by scoring two crackers on his full debut in an FA Cup replay against Oxford. Spent the end of last season on loan at Crystal Palace.

Sam Dalla Bona

The six-footer was snapped up by Chelsea from Serie B club Atalanta's youth set-up in July 1997, even though he'll only celebrate his twentieth birthday in February 2001. Has captained the Italy U-18 team, and in his first full season in England he scored an impressive 16 goals from midfield for the reserves.

Carlos Marinelli

Dubbed the 'new Maradona' the Argentinian signed for Middlesbrough, aged 17, for around £1.25m in September 1999. He was spotted playing against Boro for Buenos Aries club Boca Juniors in the Milk Cup (a prestigious youth tournament in Ireland). The attacking midfielder made an immediate impact, netting five goals in his first seven games for the youths and reserves. He made his Boro debut as a substitute against Sheffield Wednesday in December 1999.

Joe Cole

The Londoner, despite not being 20 until November 2001, is a regular fixture in the West Ham side. The midfielder has progressed to England U-21 level, and is being touted as the best England player in his position since Paul Gascoigne. His quick feet and audacious approach have already embarrassed many a Premiership defender.

Jermaine Pennant

The right-sided midfielder will only be 18 in January, but has already been the subject of a transfer reported to be worth £2m, when he left Notts County for Arsenal in January 1999. Capped at U-15 and U-16 level, he became Arsenal's youngest-ever player when he came on as a substitute, aged 16 years, 10 months and 15 days, at Middlesbrough in the Worthington Cup in November 1999.

Jay Bothroyd

A left-footed centre-forward who will be 19 in May 2001. Born in Islington, he has represented England at U-15, U-16 and U-18 level and joined Arsenal in 1998. Unfortunately, he has since left the famous North London side.

John Halls

A versatile, technically proficient player who turns 19 in February 2001. Comfortable at centre-back, right-back or in midfield, he joined Arsenal in the summer of 1998. Born in Islington, he played for Islington/Camden in the 1997 English Schools Trophy final. Has England caps at U-17 and U-18 level.

Stephen Bywater

Born in Manchester, the West Ham goalkeeper will be 20 in June 2001. He made his Premiership debut in spectacular circumstances, coming on to replace the injured Shaka Hislop in the Hammers' 5-4 victory over Bradford City in February 2000. Spent time on loan at Wycombe last season (1999-00), having also helped West Ham United to a Youth league and cup double the previous season.

Paul Konchesky

Attacking left-back who is regularly involved with Charlton's first team squad. He became Charlton's youngest-ever player at 16 years and 93 days in a home win over Oxford in August 1997, and made his Premiership debut against Newcastle in January 2000. An England Under-18 regular, he will celebrate his 20th birthday in May 2001.

Gary McSheffrey

Forward who, at 16 years and 198 days, became Coventry's youngest-ever player when he came on as a substitute in a 4-1 win over Aston Villa in February 1999. Is regularly involved in the Sky Blues' first team squad after impressing in the FA Youth Cup final defeat by West Ham in May 1999. Will turn 20 in August 2001.

Chris Kirkland

Coventry goalkeeper who saved a penalty in the first leg of the FA Youth Cup final in 1999, although he went on to finish on the losing side. Was involved with Coventry's first team squad and England U-18s last season. At 6'3", his physical presence is a definite advantage for a player who won't be 20 until May 2001.

Gareth Barry

Even though he won't turn 20 until February, he is already a regular in the Aston Villa team and made his full England debut, as a sub, in a friendly match played before England's Euro 2000 campaign, when he was a squad member. A one-time captain of England U-18s and also a member of the U-21s, coach Kevin Keegan sees him as the vital part of his bid to play a left footed wing-back. Although he also plays in this position for Aston Villa, he is equally comfortable in midfield. Signed a five-year contract with Villa in February 1999.

Jermaine Defoe

Quick and skilful, Defoe made an appearance on the West Ham bench at Newcastle, in January 2000. A prolific scorer, he is a graduate of the FA's School of Excellence, and has represented England at U-15, U-16 and U-18 levels. Will be 19 in October 2001.

Jamie McMaster

An attacking midfielder noted for his stamina, he was born in Sydney, Australia, but holds a British passport (which qualifies him to play for any of the four home nations). A unofficial 1993 agreement between England, Scotland, Wales and Northern Ireland states that precedence is given to the country with which a player has a direct bloodline. Given McMaster's father is from Glasgow, Scotland say he should play for them, but England have included him in their U-18 squad. He'll be 19 in November 2001, but has already played for Leeds Reserves.

Jlloyd Samuel

Born in Trinidad, he joined Aston Villa on a Youth Training Scheme in 1997, having previously been on Charlton's books. A centre-back who can play anywhere across the back line, he made his full Villa debut as a substitute in their Worthington Cup defeat at Chester in September 1999. A regular in the England youth ranks, the defender will be 20 in March 2001.

Stuart Parnaby

A product of the FA's National School of Excellence, before the set-up was moved away from Lilleshall, he is a mature centre-back who has represented England at U-15, U-16 and U-18 level. Currently at Middlesbrough, Stuart Parnaby will turn 19 in July 2001.

Peter Clarke

Born in Southport, he joined Everton as a trainee. Has represented both England U-16s and England U-18s and is regularly involved in Walter Smith's 16 for Premiership games. Captained Everton's U-19 side in 1999-00 from centre-back. Will celebrate his 19th birthday in January 2001.

Francis Jeffers

Became only the second 16-year-old ever to play

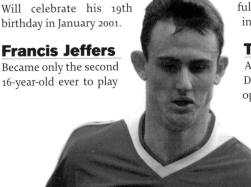

for Everton's first team, when he came on as a substitute away at Manchester United in December 1997. Suffered a major set-back with a mystery heart virus, but since then he's started regularly for the Toffees, banging in a hat-full of goals and impressing everybody with his pace and finishing. Scored on his U-21 debut for England, and was called into the full England squad for the friendly in Hungary in April 1999. Turns 20 in January 2001.

Terry Dunfield

Although born in Canada, midfielder Terry Dunfield excelled at an England youth development course in La Manga, Spain, and has represented England at U-18 level. He has impressed at Manchester City youths with his technical proficiency and two-footedness, and will only be 19 in February.

Richard Logan

Strong and quick, he made his Ipswich Town debut against Grimsby Town in January 1999, after which he signed professional forms for the club. Having been picked for the England U-18s, coach Martin Hunter said he had the potential to become a "good old-fashioned centre-forward." He turns 19 in January 2001.

Matthew Harmshaw

Born on New Year's Day 1982, he is a very direct winger who can play on either flank. Has represented England U-18s, and played in the U-16 European Championship in 1999. Has played regularly for Sheffield Wednesday reserves, and was occasionally involved in the Owls' Premiership 16 last season.

Adam Murray

Birmingham-born midfielder spotted by Derby scout Les Dolphin at the age of 12. The only player to feature at all levels for the Rams in 1998-99 (Youth, Reserves and full Senior squad). He broke into the first team against West Ham and picked up Derby's Young Player of the Year Award. Will turn 20 in September 2001.

Mark Maley

Has been capped by his country at U-15, U-16 and U-18 levels and made his debut for Sunderland – despite hailing from Tyneside – in the Worthington Cup against York City in August 1998. Comfortable at either right-back or centre-back he'll turn 20 in January 2001.

Ian Murray

Born in Edinburgh, he signed schoolboy forms for Dundee United, but moved to Hibernian in 1998. Since then he has featured in their first team squad, and has also been selected for Scotland U-18s. The midfielder will celebrate his 20th birthday in March 2001.

Tom McManus

The Glasgow-born forward is frequently involved in Hibs' first team squad, making his debut as a substitute in a 4-0 win over Stranraer in May 1999. Has earned selection for Scotland U-18s and will blow out 20 candles on his birthday cake in February 2001.

Gary Caldwell

Joined Newcastle as an intermediate in August 1997 and turned professional in August 1999, impressing in several reserve games in the first half of the season. Was included in the squad that travelled to the Olympic Stadium in Rome for a UEFA Cup third round first-leg match. The defender has represented Scotland at U-18 level, and will be 19 in April 2001.

Chris Doig

The defender made his Nottingham Forest debut on Boxing Day 1998 at Old Trafford, having previously represented Queen of the South at the age of 16. Involved with Scotland at U-18 level, he will lose his teenage status in February 2001.

Mark Brown

One of Scotland's most promising 'keepers, he will celebrate his 20th birthday in February 2001. He has represented Scotland at U-18 level and despite the presence of such 'keepers as Klos, Charbonnier and Niemi at Ibrox, he still commands a regular place in the Rangers' reserve squad.

Here's your big chance to win a super prize in our great MOTD easy to enter competition ...

First Prize

relive those great match moments with the Match of the Day Football Table, featuring: 22 chunky style players, grass effect pitch, ball launcher, scoring system and removable, anti-slip legs.

Plus 6 Second Prizes

of MOTD footballs signed by the presenters.

Plus 100 Runners-Up Prizes

of posters of MOTD's top 100 players.

How to Enter:

All you have to do is answer this simple question:

"In which season was 'Match of the Day' first screened?"

Write your answer on a postcard or the back of a sealed envelope (don't forget to include your name, address and age) and post to:

'Match of the Day Competition'
Egmont World Ltd.,
Deanway Technology Centre,
Wilmslow Road,
Handforth,
Cheshire SK9 3FB.
(Closing date for entries 26 January 2001)

Rules

- 1/ 107 winners will be chosen at random and notified by post.
- 2/ Judges' decision will be final. No correspondence will be entered into.
- 3/ The winners' names will be made available from Egmont World Ltd (on request) after 5 February 2001. Please enclose a stamped addressed envelope.
- 4/ Employees (and their relatives) of Egmont World Ltd and their associated companies are not eligible to enter.
- 5/ Entries are limited to one per person.
- 6/ Competition is open to residents of the UK, Channel Isles and Ireland only.
- 7/ The Publishers reserve the right to vary prizes, subject to availability.
- 8/ Closing date for entries is 26 January 2001.

Match Fit
MOTD

Devised and Drawn by Paul Trevillion

IT is a medical fact there are close links between physical health, physical fitness and mental alertness.

These are the essential attributes necessary to enable a player to compete well in the demanding pace of the modern game, with its interchanging tactics and rigorous physical challenges.

At any level, at any age, you need to be fit in order to compete well. Fitness gives you confidence, suppleness and the competitive edge.

The three S's – Suppleness, Speed and Skill are necessary to get the best possible performance out of your natural ability and for you to play to your full potential.

Warming Up before a match and Warming Down after the contest are vital in the modern game, with the fitness coaches and physios all doing stretching work with their players pre and post match.

Over the following pages we look at the basic ways to improve your balance, suppleness and fitness and outline what they involve. Use at least some of these to gently warm up before you take to the field of play.

Warm Up Exercises

Warm up exercises are an essential preparation for the game of football. Fifteen minutes of gentle warm ups will increase your heart rate and pump blood to the muscles where it will soon be needed.

1 POSTURE

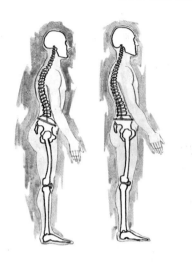

Poor posture means insufficient breathing – so, like Michael Owen in full flow, keep your shoulders back and maintain your full height.

2 WAIST SWIVEL

Stand tall with feet slightly wider than your hips. Have your knees flexed. Turn round to the side keeping your hips facing forward. Return to centre and repeat opposite side. Breathe easily throughout.
REPEAT 15 TIMES

● Note how Ed De Goey uses his waist muscles when stretching for shots.

3 BACK BENDS

Stand tall with your feet slightly wider than your hips. Bend from the waist and touch the floor. Keeping your arms fully stretched, stand up straight and bend backwards, letting your arms stretch upwards and beyond your head. Breathe easily throughout.
REPEAT 10 TIMES

4 PRESS-UPS

Lie face down on the ground, raise your body up until your arms are straight then lower again. Concentrate on keeping your body horizontal and your back straight. Breathe easily throughout.
**START at 5 PRESS-UPS,
THEN MOVE YOUR TARGET TO 10, 15, etc**

● Extravagant goal celebration leaps are all part of the fun. But don't pull a muscle, be fit like Dwight Yorke.

5 SIT-UPS

Lie on your back with your knees bent – feet flat on floor – with your hands behind the base of your head. Lift your head, shoulders and torso slowly off the floor and touch your knees with your elbows. When lifting and lowering the

Match Fit
 is part of the MOTD logo

body, concentrate on using the abdominal muscles, avoiding any unnecessary strain on the back. Breathe easily throughout.
REPEAT 10 TIMES

6 SQUAT THRUSTS

Lie face down on the ground, raise your body up with your arms until they are straight. From this position bring both your legs forward in one movement. Then push both your feet back out together. Breathe easily throughout.
REPEAT 10 TIMES

● Tore Andre Flo has great mental alertness. Mind and body fitness means he's always looking for the half-chance – and ready to punish it.

7 LEG STRETCH

Stand straight with your legs wide apart. Bend each leg alternately by adopting a gentle lunging position as in fencing. Keep your non-bending leg straight. At the same time lower your body towards the floor. Hold for a count of FIVE. Relax and repeat with the other leg. Breathe easily throughout.
REPEAT 10 TIMES ON EACH SIDE

8 HAMSTRING STRETCH

Lie on your back with your legs fully stretched. Lift one leg, keeping your toes bent (not pointing) and gently, with a straight leg, reach back towards the head. Exert a little pressure to move your foot further forwards towards your head. Gently lower your leg to the ground and repeat with your other leg. Breathe easily throughout.
REPEAT 10 TIMES

● Patrick Vieira's legs seem almost like elastic when he stretches out to win the ball.

All exercises should be undertaken with qualified adult supervision.

OVERVIEW

SOL CAMPBELL

- Good Posture
- Shoulders Back
- Maintaining Full Height
- Shoulder Turn
- Waist-Swivel Hips
- Facing Forward

LEEDS' HARRY KEWELL

Demonstrates the leg stretch. His famous Kangaroo Leap goal celebrations also illustrate the amazing strength in his legs

Michael Owen in full flow

WEST HAM'S PAOLO DI CANIO

Has great poise and grace. And his pre-match hamstring stretches helped him score a wonder goal against Wimbledon last season

PAUL SCHOLES

The superfit Man United midfield genius Paul Scholes has the three S's – Suppleness, Speed, Skill ... plus Stamina. It's a match-winning combination!

Who am I?

Can you name the famous player from the following picture clues of items found at his home, and his home ground?

This player has a great fondness for the gee-gees, being the part-owner of several racehorses. He's had plenty of winners, too.

Born in Dublin in 1966, he's been a leading light up front for the Republic of Ireland since gaining his first cap for his country in 1986. Some might say he's as tall as a lamp-post, too.

His former clubs include a pair of giants in the game – Arsenal and Manchester City. Last season, he formed a little and large striking partnership which opposition defences didn't find funny at all.

The player's current home ground is one of the newest in the Premier League, the club having only moved there in 1997. It is located in an area that's a real hotbed of football. The fans inside the ground had plenty to celebrate last season, with the team performing wonderfully well on its return to the Premiership.

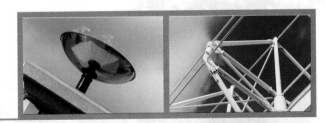

▲ NIALL QUINN

At Liverpool, they've got Didi Hamann who cost £8million, and Steven Gerrard who cost nothing. Over at Leeds, they've just snapped up Mark Viduka for more than £7million, and they've got Stephen McPhail who cost nothing. Down in London, Chelsea signed Jimmy Floyd Hasselbaink in the summer for a cool £12million, and they've got John Harley who cost - you guessed it - nothing. Gerrard, McPhail and Harley all came through the youth development schemes at their clubs, and clearly the soccer academies the leading clubs are currently setting up could save them fortunes in transfer fees in the future. So what is it like to be at one? What do young players learn at these centres of excellence, and what is demanded of them in return? MOTD Annual had a chat with two soccer-mad South London brothers to find out.

WILL CHAPMAN, 12 in September 2000, plays wide-midfield or full-back, and has a tasty left foot. Younger brother BEN was 10, also in September, and can play up front or in midfield. Both are registered players with Fulham – in fact Ben was the youngest player they'd ever taken on when he joined the club at just 8 years old. They are being taught to play the game on an improved level, and to develop good footballing habits. Already the coaching has had a huge effect. "Before, when I was playing for my local team," says Will, "we all just tended to chase the ball. Now we're thinking much more about where the ball is going to go, where we should be on the pitch. It's a much better standard of play."

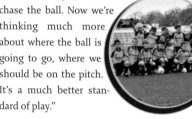

At Will and Ben's age, the players have two training sessions a week, lasting one-and-a-half hours, and then there will usually be a match on the Sunday. The games are against other football club academy teams, including sides from London, Bristol and Southampton. From the age of 13, there's a third weekly training session as well.

All sessions start with warm-ups and stretches. Then there'll be skill drills of various kinds, such as running with the ball, shooting practice, even work on set pieces. The sessions end with practice matches, when the coaches are looking for the players to use what they've learnt from the drills in game situa-tions. There can also be homework, too. "They might tell us to work at home on your weaker foot, or on heading," Ben points out. Will has even been asked to write up what happened during training to help get the session's messages across.

Matches against other academies at Will and Ben's level are on shorter pitches with perhaps 8 or 9-a-side. They are played over four quarters of 15 minutes, or sometimes three periods of 20 minutes. Proper 11-a-side games on full size pitches start for 12-year-olds, when players can also be offered contracts - as long as four years in some cases - to stay with the Academy. Interestingly, though, it is stressed to the players that how they play in a game is far more important than winning it. This can put the coaches at odds with parents watching from the sidelines, who are all eager for their children to come out on top, but they stick to their guns. "The coaches are sometimes more pleased if you've performed well and lost, than if you've not played too well yet won," Will points out. Underlining this is the fact that there are no cups or medals to be won playing Academy matches.

The number of games a season the boys are allowed to play is at the moment limited to 30, to guard against them playing too much football too early. "You can balance up the number of Academy games by playing matches for your school," the boys add, but they are not allowed to play for other teams.

Occasionally, they get to play at some famous places, such as Craven Cottage and Bisham Abbey, where England train. "Going down the tunnel at Craven Cottage was really exciting," says Ben. "But I got a bit nervous and didn't play my best. I did much better at Bisham Abbey."

They bump into Fulham's first team players from time to time at training, although they are usually very busy. But former Fulham manager Paul Bracewell used to watch the Academy players train quite a bit, as did Karlheinz Riedle when he took over, although Ben points out, "His son plays in the same team as me."

As Academy players, the boys receive free tickets for every Fulham home match. They are also given about £200 worth of clothing, including a track-suit, wet weather top and club t-shirts. But, in return, certain standards of behaviour are demanded – they must wear club track-suits and arrive an hour before kick-off when playing academy matches for example. There is a book of etiquette outlining what is expected of academy players.

There is rigorous testing of fitness levels, too, and the players are very aware that they are being monitored all the time, even in the simplest of passing exercises. When errors occur they are pointed out immediately, with practice matches stopped if necessary. Feelings aren't spared, either. Players in all age groups are told if they are falling short of what is required. "Having the right attitude is very important," says Will, and the pair know of youngsters who were at Fulham and who, despite being terrific players, have been released.

Will and Ben also know that the failure rate is very high. Yet while the brothers are aware of the pitfalls, the confidence they've gained from quality coaching at the Academy dispels any fear of failure. "I want to play for England, with my brother," confirms Ben with total conviction when asked about his ambitions.

So after the Charltons and the Nevilles, it could be the Chapmans, because while Will and Ben refuse to rule it out, neither should we ...

Academies
MOTD

Having produced players of the calibre of Frank Lampard, Rio Ferdinand and more recently Joe Cole and Michael Carrick, West Ham United is one of the top talent-creators in the Premiership. MOTD Annual has been given permission to peek into the club's excellent Academy Brochure. Take a look at the following Players' Guide, then ask yourself ... could you fit in?

CODE OF CONDUCT
– PLAYERS' GUIDE

Players are reminded that they represent West Ham United Football Academy and should behave in an appropriate manner.

Players are required to wear Club track-suits for all matches unless otherwise instructed by their group coaches.

Swearing, fighting, bullying and bad behaviour of any kind will not be tolerated.

Shower facilities are always available both at training and matches. Players will be encouraged to shower after training/playing, so please provide alternative clothing to change into, particularly in adverse weather conditions.

Players should attend all Club sessions in the Club training kit, which must be clean and smart in appearance. Training kit is not to be worn for social purposes.

All match kit will be provided. This must be returned immediately after the game, turned the right way out.

Players should attend both training and matches with clean boots/training shoes. Jewellery must not be worn for matches or training sessions for personal safety and that of other players. The Club will not accept responsibility for jewellery or valuables brought to training sessions or matches.

All Academy members are expected to keep themselves fit at all times through a sensible, nourishing diet, exercise, appropriate rest and the strict avoidance of alcohol and tobacco.

When travelling to away fixtures players should travel on the away team bus with the official team party – unless prior permission has been obtained. Players may go home with parents/guardians as long as the team coach has been informed.

For all home matches, players should arrive 60 minutes before kick-off time. For away matches players should arrive 15 minutes before the designated leaving time. Under no circumstances should players argue or

Stephen McPhail

dispute decisions by referees or their assistants. Players must make a commitment to academic achievement and adhere strictly to their individual programmes at school.

Although the Academy regime can be tough, top managers, youth team coaches and professional players will always impress on youngsters that football is supposed to be a fun sport, and MOTD Annual fully endorses this viewpoint.

Many of you will not be of the standard to make it into the Academy set-ups, but that does not necessarily mean you are a bad football player. Whatever talent for kicking and heading the ball you have, always try to remember to play football to the best of your ability and with a smile on your face. That way you will never let anyone down.

Michael Carrick

In another trip down football's memory lane, MOTD Annual presents the ups and the downs, the highs and the lows, the joys and the blows, of the seasons since BBC TV's programme was first screened ...

1964-65

Sir Stanley Matthews retires, aged 50. The Wizard of Dribble's final game for Stoke City is a special 'benefit' match versus an International XI.

Spurs and Scotland midfield star John White killed by lightning at a golf course while sheltering from rain.

...n professional footballers are sent to jail for match 'fixing'.

West Ham triumph at Wembley beating Munich 1860 2-0 to lift the European Cup Winners' Cup.

1965-66

When Charlton's Keith Peacock runs on to the pitch in August, he becomes the first-ever player to appear as a substitute.

Prior to the World Cup being played in this country, the trophy is stolen when on show at a stamp exhibition. It is later unearthed hidden in a paper bag by a black and white mongrel dog called Pickles.

There are fans on the Wembley pitch as Geoff Hurst scores his third and England's fourth goal in a dramatic extra-time World Cup Final victory against West Germany. Minutes later captain Bobby Moore holds aloft the Jules Rimet trophy – the first and only time England have won the World Cup.

1966-67

England manager Alf Ramsey is knighted in the New Year's Honours' list.

In the first all London FA Cup Final of the century, Spurs beat Chelsea 2-1.

Celtic are the 'Kings of Europe' as they beat Inter Milan in Lisbon to become the first British side to win the European Cup.

Alan Ball costs Everton £110,000 when they sign the little midfielder from Blackpool ... the first six-figure transfer agreed between British clubs.

1967-68

In the Charity Shield Spurs' goalie Pat Jennings scores directly with his 'up-and-under' penalty-area clearance.

With minutes remaining Benfica's Eusebio is through on goal and shoots, but Man United's goalie Alex Stepney flings himself heroically at the ball and the danger is over ... the 1968 European Cup Final played at Wembley will go into extra-time. Goals from Best, Kidd and Charlton wrap it up for the 'Red Devils' and manager Matt Busby turns the tragedy of Munich 1958 into the European Cup triumph of 1968.

Playing against a ruthless Yugoslavia, Alan Mullery becomes the first-ever England player to be sent-off in a full international fixture.

Italy win the 1968 European Championships.

1968-69

Celtic achieve their second-ever domestic 'treble' ... winning the League, SFA Cup and League Cup.

Northampton complete an incredible cycle of ups and downs ... going from Div 4 in 1960 to Div 1 in 1965 and back to Div 4 in 1969.

George Best is voted European Footballer of the Year.

Led by Bobby Moncur, Newcastle beat Ujpest Dozsa and win the Inter-Cities Fairs Cup over two legs.

1969-70

Bobby Charlton wins his 100th England cap. He later went on to surpass Billy Wright's record of 105 caps.

There are scenes of rejoicing in Brazil when Pele scores his 1,000th first-class goal.

Returning from suspension, Man United's George Best hits six goals in a Cup match v Northampton.

Man City take the European Cup Winners' Cup, beating Gornik Zabrze.

Brazil win the 1970 World Cup as holders England go down in a memorable quarter-final match v West Germany.

1970-71

Mighty Leeds crash out of the FA Cup against Div 4's lowly Colchester.

In the New Year's fixture between Rangers and Celtic, 66 fans are tragically killed when barriers collapse at Ibrox Park.

It's 'double' joy for Arsenal as they become only the second English side to win both the Championship and the FA Cup in the same season.

Leeds win the Inter-Cities and Chelsea the Cup Winners' Cup against Europe's best.

1971-72

Bournemouth's Ted MacDougall sets a scoring record in the FA Cup when he hits nine goals against non-league Margate.

Inspired by Footballer of the Year Gordon Banks and midfield maestro George Eastham, Stoke City win their only ever major honour – the League Cup.

It's an all-England UEFA Cup Final as Spurs defeat Wolves over two legs.

West Germany win the European Championships.

1972-73

England goalkeeper Gordon Banks loses the sight in his right eye after his car is involved in a head-on collision.

Another England World Cup winner, Man United's Bobby Charlton, announces his retirement from the game he has graced.

England captain Bobby Moore celebrates his century of international caps.

Div Two side Sunderland record a brilliant FA Cup Final win over odds-on favourites Leeds United. Goalie Jim Montgomery is the hero of the hour.

Liverpool win the UEFA Cup to take their first European title.

1973-74
Three up/three down promotion and relegation is introduced.

England fail to qualify for the World Cup Finals when Poland hold them to a 1-1 draw at Wembley.

 Sir Alf Ramsey is sacked as England boss.

Leeds win the Championship and Liverpool the FA Cup.

Man United are relegated.

Despite a 0-0 result against Brazil, Scotland are knocked out in the early stages of the World Cup Finals and hosts West Germany go on to win the new-look 'ice-cream cone' trophy.

1974-75
In a tale of four managers, Don Revie becomes the new England supremo; Brian Clough is sacked by Leeds after just 44 days; and two greats, Liverpool's Bill Shankly and Tottenham's Bill Nicholson, announce their retirements.

 Malcolm Macdonald becomes the first England player to score five goals in a Wembley international.

Celtic's League supremacy comes to an end when Rangers end their nine-year reign at the top of Scottish football.

1975-76
Jimmy Hill, managing-director of Coventry City, announces he has become Saudi Arabia's London-based soccer supremo.

Liverpool lift the League Championship plus

 the UEFA Cup and little Kevin Keegan is crowned Footballer of the Year.

In a penalty shoot-out, Czechoslovakia win a dramatic European Championship Final against West Germany. Wales are eliminated in the quarter-finals.

1976-77
 On 2nd October 1976 red and yellow cards are introduced.

After a record-breaking 824 League appearances – 713 for Southampton and 111 for Hereford – ex-England winger Terry Paine retires at the end of the season.

Bobby Moore plays his 1,000th first-class game, wearing Fulham's colours. He retires soon after.

After 13 consecutive seasons in Europe, Liverpool are rewarded when they win their first European Cup Final against Borussia Moenchengladbach.

1977-78
The High Court upholds the FA's ban on 12-year-old Theresa Bennett from playing for a boys' team.

Rangers capture all three trophies in Scotland.

Bobby Robson masterminds Ipswich's first-ever FA Cup Final victory.

Liverpool lift the European Cup for the second year in succession.

 Argentina win the World Cup and Spurs swoop for two of their stars, Osvaldo Ardiles and Ricardo Villa.

1978-79
 Viv Anderson becomes the first black footballer to represent England in a full international.

The FA impose a 10-year ban on ex-England manager Don Revie for bringing the game into disrepute .

A headed goal by Trevor Francis wins Nott'm Forest the European Cup. Three months before, manager Brian Clough had made Francis Britain's first £1m player.

Playing for SV Hamburg, Kevin Keegan is voted European Footballer of the Year.

1979-80
Manager Alex Ferguson ends the Old Firm's monopoly as Aberdeen win the Scottish League Championship.

Wolves spend £1.4m on Andy Gray.

 A rare headed goal from West Ham's Trevor Brooking beats Arsenal in the FA Cup Final.

Nott'm Forest make it a 'double' in the European Cup when, for the second season in a row, they record a 1-0 win – this time against Hamburg.

1980-81
Bottom of the table Leicester City destroy Liverpool's 85 game unbeaten home sequence at Anfield.

Sunday football reappears as Darlington entertain Mansfield.

For the fifth year in a row an English side is victorious in the European Cup when Liverpool defeat Real Madrid. Ipswich make it a glorious home 'double' by lifting the UEFA Cup.

1981-82
The Football League introduces three points for a win.

 Bobby Robson is appointed England manager.

Liverpool's legendary Bill Shankly dies from a heart attack.

Aston Villa beat Bayern Munich to record yet another European Cup win for an English club.

The World Cup tournament is held in sunny Spain and Italy beat West Germany in the Final.

1982-83

The man with the big hands, goalkeeper Pat Jennings, reaches his 1,000th senior appearance

Aberdeen and Dundee United upstage the 'big two' with the Dons winning the European Cup Winners' Cup and the Terrors clinching the Scottish Championship.

Dropped by England manager Bobby Robson, Newcastle's Kevin Keegan announces that his international career is over.

1983-84

Spurs beat Nott'm Forest in the first of 10 'live' League matches to be shown on TV.

Aged 16 years and 57 days, Ipswich Town's Jason Dozell becomes the youngest goalscorer in First Division history.

Michel Platini's nine goals help host nation France to win the European Championships.

1984-85

A season of disasters. On May 11th at Bradford City's Valley Parade, 56 fans die when the club's wooden stand catches fire. Then, 18 days later, before the European Cup Final can be played between Liverpool and Juventus at the Heysel Stadium in Brussels, 39 football supporters are tragically killed. As a result UEFA bans all English clubs from future European competition.

England defeat Turkey 8-0 in Istanbul.

Everton win two big trophies, the Division One title and the European Cup Winners' Cup.

1985-86

In their first-ever season in Division One, Oxford United win the League Cup Final.

In the summer of '86, Liverpool's Ian Rush negotiates a £3m deal with Juventus and will play for them the following season. Gary Lineker joins Barcelona for £4.2m.

Gary Lineker's six goals make him top scorer in the 1986 World Cup Finals. England are beaten in the quarter-finals by Maradona's infamous 'Hand of God' goal.

1986-87

Alex Ferguson's managerial reign starts at Man United.

Coventry goalkeeper Steve Ogrizovic scores with a long clearance against Sheffield Wednesday.

The first-ever play-offs bring joy and sadness to the participating clubs.

1987-88

At 17 years and 240 days, Alan Shearer is the youngest player to score a hat-trick in the First Division when Southampton beat Arsenal 4-2.

Goalie Peter Shilton breaks the League's record appearance total when he plays in his 825th match.

Wimbledon's Dave Beasant's penalty-save and a goal from Lawrie Sanchez are enough to defeat Liverpool in the FA Cup Final.

With Ruud Gullit in outstanding form, Holland win the 1988 Euro Championships.

1988-89

In the FA Cup semi-final between Liverpool and Nott'm Forest played at Hillsborough, a crowd surge at the Leppings Lane end of

the stadium results in 96 spectators tragically losing their lives. Subsequently, an inquiry is set-up and its conclusions recommend all-seater stadia.

Mark Lawrenson is fired from the manager's seat at Oxford.

Brighton goalkeeper Perry Digweed fails to turn up for a match because no-one remembered to tell him he was playing.

High drama at Liverpool when Arsenal win the Championship with a late, late Michael Thomas goal.

1989-90

Juventus break the world transfer record when they sign Roberto Baggio for £7.7m.

Paul Gascoigne's tears are not enough to stop England going out at the semi-final stage of the 1990 World Cup – beaten by eventual winners West Germany in a penalty shoot-out.

Bobby Robson resigns as England manager and Aston Villa's Graham Taylor takes over.

1990-91

The ban on English clubs competing in Europe is lifted.

Gary Lineker wins FIFA's £20,000 fair play prize for never being booked or sent off during his career.

Kenny Dalglish retires after his 516th appearance for Liverpool.

Paul Gascoigne self-destructs in the FA Cup Final, badly injuring himself. Spurs beat Forest 2-1.

Man United conquer mighty Barcelona in the European Cup Winners' Cup Final to make it a triumphant return for English clubs to European competition.

1991-92

Kevin Keegan takes over at Newcastle and rescues the club from relegation to the Third Division.

Beaten by Sweden, England crash out of the European Championships, a tournament eventually won by Denmark.

1992-93

England's 1966 World Cup-winning captain Bobby Moore loses his battle with cancer. The football world mourns the untimely death of one of its greatest players and ambassadors of the game. At his West Ham United club, the Stadium forecourt is a sea of flowers and messages as the fans pay a tearful tribute to their hero.

Brian Clough bows out of football waving a fond farewell to Nott'm Forest fans.

Rangers do the 'treble' in Scotland.

Man United win the first Premiership title with 84 points.

1993-94

Graham Taylor's England fail to qualify for the 1994 World Cup Finals and Terry Venables is subsequently appointed England's new team boss.

Two Eric Cantona penalties help Man United to a 4-0 FA Cup victory and the Old Trafford club complete the 'double'.

Liverpool demolish the world-famous Kop at the end of the season.

The World Cup returns to Brazil after 24 years when they beat Italy – the first Final to be decided on a penalty shoot-out.

1994-95

After being red-carded, Man United's Eric Cantona tackles a Crystal Palace fan as he leaves the pitch.

Overseas players score a unique double when Jurgen Klinsmann takes England's Footballer of the Year award and Brian Laudrup wins the two top Scottish awards.

Blackburn thrillingly win the League title when, on the last day of the season, they just pip Man United to the trophy.

1995-96

The Bosman ruling comes into effect, when the European Court of Justice decides that free movement of players must exist between European clubs within the European Community.

Mick McCarthy replaces Jack Charlton as the manager of the Republic of Ireland.

In a race to the wire, Man United clinch another Championship and then lift the FA Cup with a solitary goal from Eric Cantona.

Gareth Southgate misses his penalty-kick against eventual winners Germany in the semi-final of the European Championships and England are out of the tournament.

1996-97

Newcastle break the bank to sign Alan Shearer from Blackburn Rovers for £15m.

Under-11 boys' team Warren Wanderers are deducted 30 points for fielding players who are five months too old.

Peter Shilton records his 1,000th League game playing for Leyton Orient against Brighton.

Chelsea director Matthew Harding is killed in a helicopter crash.

1997-98

Michael Owen becomes the youngest England international of the 20th Century when he plays against Chile, aged 18 years and 59 days. In the World Cup Finals played in France later that year, he will score a wonder goal against Argentina at the quarter-final stage.

It's Arsenal's 'double' as Arséne Wenger's team sweeps all before them.

France win the 1998 World Cup, beating a below-par Brazil in the Final.

1998-1999

Having made the decision the previous season, the top 10 Scottish clubs kick-off in their first-ever Premier League.

Glenn Hoddle leaves the England manager's job to be replaced by Kevin Keegan.

Sir Alf Ramsey dies.

On the 16th May, Man United claim the Premiership title, on the 22nd they beat Newcastle to win the FA Cup and on the 26th they dramatically defeat Bayern Munich to snatch the European Champions Cup. An amazing treble.

Liverpool's Steve McManaman agrees a five-year contract with Real Madrid.

1999-2000

Man United announce their temporary withdrawal from the FA Cup competition.

Sir Stanley Matthews dies.

Barcelona and Real Madrid knock out Chelsea and Man United respectively at the quarter-final stage of the European Champions League. Real Madrid go on to win the prestigious competition

Man United, Arsenal and Leeds will represent England in the 2000-01 European Champions League.

France defeat Italy 2-1 to win Euro 2000.

'NOTHING SURPRISES ME IN FOOTBALL' *It's a familiar saying in the game, often used by Sunderland manager Peter Reid for one. But given some of the things footballers get up to off the pitch – a selection of which MOTD Annual presents here – maybe there's still plenty going on to raise even Reidie's eyebrows ...*

A few footballers over the years have turned to music to help them relax. To name two of the current crop, there's Dion Dublin with his saxophone, and Nolberto Solano with his trumpet. Neil Sullivan's choice is a wind instrument, too, but oddly it's not the bagpipes for Scotland's Number One. No ... as you do, he's gone for a didgeridoo ...

SURPRISE RATING: 6/10

You can only assume that 'Razor' Ruddock asked for too much money to pose for this pic. "That Steve Stone – some of the things he does in shaving. Unbelievable."

SURPRISE RATING: 5/10

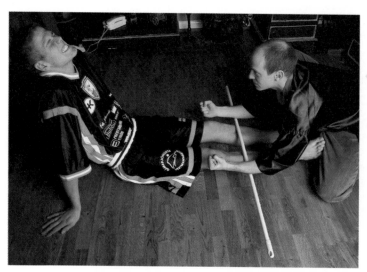

"That Hermann Hreidarsson – some of the things he does in training. Unbelievable." Here, the Icelandic international is on the receiving end of a shin-conditioning exercise suggested by martial arts' expert Matt Gross. The technique – rolling a wooden pole up and down the shins and exerting a sensible level of pressure - is used by Kung Fu fighters to increase their tolerance to blows on that part of the leg. While shinpads should always be worn, Matt believes that similar occasional shin-conditioning could benefit footballers – and Hermann's in no position to argue.

SURPRISE RATING: 8/10

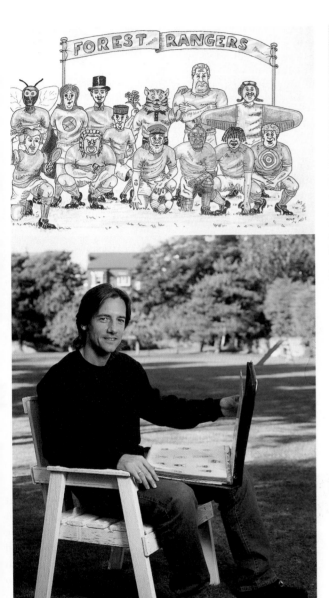

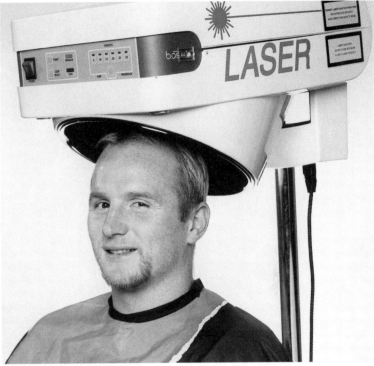

What's this? Hardman John Hartson under the hairdryer? Some mistake, surely – at best, and we're being kind here, he's a touch thin on top. Not exactly the sort to trouble the barber at all. Ah, but here's a strange thing – he might be doing so in the future, for this is the Welsh striker undergoing some laser-powered hair restoration treatment. It seems to be working very well on his chin, anyway ...

SURPRISE RATING: 7/10

Move over Melchester Rovers, here's another side which on paper could be devastating. Forest Rangers boast, among others, a cat-like 'keeper, a flying winger, a target man up front and a magician in midfield. The curious thing is, the detailed drawings and sharply devised characters are in fact the creations of artful midfielder Ian Bishop.

SURPRISE RATING: 9/10

 Ball jugglers. Two-a penny these days. Every club has got one. But put a fruit juggler like Tony, demonstrating his Adams' apple trick, at the core of your defence, and you'll soon peel away from the rest and climb to the top of the football tree.

SURPRISE RATING: 6/10

They played at opposite ends of their teams, so it's no surprise to find that Alan and Gary are often at odds with each other when it comes to the art of scoring. They see different things when they look at the same goal, because …

Hansen hates strikers … Lineker loves 'em!

GOALS. We can't live without them. Great goals, simple goals, ugly goals, lucky goals … football's got the lot. It's goals that count, and no matter how good the game you are watching, there is a sense of anti-climax, of something missing, if it ends up 0-0.

There's just something about that scoreline which makes you think 'dull'. But if football is about goals, it is also about opinions. Assessing the merit of a particular strike can cause heated debate, and not just amongst defenders arguing about who should have been marking the forward who scored it. It depends on your point of view: one fan's great finish might be another fan's feeble challenge.

This is the reason why, on occasions, there appears to be a certain amount of disagreement in the MOTD studios on a Saturday Night/Sunday morning. Messrs Hansen and Lineker argue their corners because they each have a different 'take' on the goals they see.

So who's right? Well, judge for yourself as we look again at three memorable strikes from the recent past, accompanied by the sort of typical contrasting assessments the pair are famous for …

The sensational solo run – Ryan Giggs for Man Utd v Arsenal, April 1999

WHEN an opposition move breaks down, the United wide-man picks up the ball in his own half, then turns on the afterburners. Carrying the ball at scintillating speed, Giggs sprints on and on, knifing into the Arsenal penalty area and, from an unfavourable angle, he crashes a thunderous left foot shot into the roof of the net.

The Hansen Analysis

'There's a lot to admire about this goal, but plenty for the opposition coaches to look at and wonder if their players couldn't have done better. First of all, there's a badly misplaced pass in midfield from Patrick Vieira which gives possession to Giggs. He reacts quickly to the gift, while no-one from Arsenal does, so he's able to get on his bike and go 20 or 30 yards before any opposition player even makes contact with him. By this stage, Giggs is flying, with only one thought in mind – getting into the opposition box. I've said it many times, defenders hate people running at them at pace, so the Arsenal back-line have got problems. But for me, they back-off and back-off, and let the United man in too easily. They offer little more than token challenges, which allow Giggs to travel all the way in virtually a straight line. Then at the end of it all, Seaman is beaten from quite a tight angle, which he might be disappointed about. Having said

Hansen v Lineker

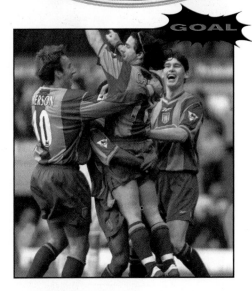

that, the sheer power of the strike is going to trouble any 'keeper. Summing up, Giggs did his job – and did it brilliantly – but for me, collectively Arsenal didn't do theirs once possession was lost.'

The Lineker Analysis

'This was Ryan Giggs at his lethal, unstoppable best. It's a fantastic goal, in which the Welshman demonstrates why he is such a phenomenal player. His control at speed is exceptional, and what speed! He covers the space between collecting the ball and firing at the target so quickly. And at the end of that lung-bursting run, he still finds the energy to unleash an explosive shot which Seaman would have done well to see, never mind save. The fact that the goal came in extra-time of a Cup semi-final replay, when United had been reduced to 10 men, just adds to its quality in my book. And let's not forget that it was scored against the famed back-line of Arsenal, not against some misfit side struggling with inexperienced defenders. The finish alone marks it out as something special, but when you consider it came at the end of a run like that, we have to be talking about one of the goals of the decade, let alone a goal of the season.'

CRISP passing and clever running from Chelsea on the opening day of last season saw Poyet steal into the Sunderland box to meet Zola's chip. His wonderfully controlled volley past the advancing 'keeper was the final touch in a sweeping move.

The Hansen Analysis

'A goal from foreign fields, this one. When Frenchman Deschamps collects the ball he is still deep in the Chelsea half. He fires a glorious long pass forward to find Zola of Italy, darting into space on the Sunderland right. Zola checks and looks up to see the Uruguayan, Poyet, making an incisive run through Sunderland's back line. Zola produces an exquisite chip over and between the defenders, right into the path of the South American's break. There's still work for Poyet to do once he's in because many a player blasts chances like this high and wide. Instead he cracks a great volley into the net. A tremendous goal, all about movement off the ball, great passing and smart finishing.'

The Lineker Analysis

'The problem with team-work goals is they tend not to get the neutral leaping out of his or her seat saying, "Did you see that?" Without doubt, Sunderland are cut apart by some classy play that makes for a picturesque goal, but while it's precise and clinical, it isn't spectacular as well. Another big factor is that it was Chelsea's fourth on the day. Sunderland, just up from Division One, had been chasing shadows all afternoon on their return to the Premiership. They'd struggled to live with their opponents, and were ready to concede to such a well-worked movement. Overall, as goals go, it's nice, it's attractive, but it's not a drop-dead stunner. Bit like me, really ..!'

The stunning strike from distance – Benito Carbone for Aston Villa v Leeds, Jan 2000

RECEIVING the ball out wide, a long way from goal, the Italian sizes up his options before shooting. He fires in a deceptively pacey curler which arcs at speed into the top corner of the net.

The Hansen Analysis

'Nigel Martyn in the Leeds goal had a wonderful season last year, but this was an embarrassing moment for him, and for the Leeds' defence in general. When the ball reaches Carbone, he's a long way out and not far from the touch-line. Fatally, no-one moves to close him down. He's got all day, it seems, to have a good long look and see what's on. By the time the Italian strikes the ball there's still no-one from Leeds within 10 yards of him. Compounding that error, Martyn drifts back towards his far post – leaving the near post unguarded – presumably because he's expecting a deep cross. It's a great hit from Carbone, who puts just the right amount of bend on the ball to whip it into the near top corner. But really, if you invite a talented player like him to take a pop at you, and grant him all the time and space he wants to pick his spot, he will do.'

The Lineker Analysis

'I think you have to give Carbone top marks for this. From an unusually wide angle, he produces a dream of a strike which relies on its subtlety as much as its power for success. Martyn looks badly out of position, but he's fooled first by the Italian disguising what he's about, and secondly by the deceptive flight of the ball. It's not so much that the 'keeper is slow to react, it's more to do with Carbone's skill in hitting the perfectly paced, perfectly curled shot.'

The intricate team move – Gus Poyet for Chelsea v Sunderland, Aug 1999

MOTD

Alan Hansen's 3 greatest goals

1 ROBERTO CARLOS

for Brazil v France, Le Tournoi 1997

2 DIEGO MARADONA

for Argentina v England, World Cup 1986

3 TREVOR SINCLAIR

for Queens Park Rangers v Barnsley, FA Cup 1997

Now let's analyse a Cup Final goal. It came in the 1986 FA Cup Final between Everton and Liverpool, following a long ball forward by the then Everton midfielder, Peter Reid. How might the pair view this one..?

The Hansen Analysis

'It was just a ball over the top for the striker to chase. Alright, the big defender was caught a bit for pace, but the striker got lucky twice with the finish. He scuffed his first effort with what was clearly his weaker left foot. This rebounded off Bruce Grobbelaar right into the striker's path for a tap-in, but even then he only just bobbled it home. An ugly goal if ever there was one.'

Gary Lineker's 3 greatest goals

1 DIEGO MARADONA

for Argentina v England, World Cup 1986

2 PAUL GASCOIGNE

for Tottenham Hotspur v Arsenal, FA Cup 1991

3 STEVE CLARIDGE

for Leicester v Middlesbrough, Coca-Cola Cup 1997

The Lineker Analysis

'A classic of its type, this one. The defender was sucked forward by the striker's movement, then he was done by the same player's spin and accelera-tion. In on goal, the striker opted to play a one-two off the 'keeper's legs before finding the net. For some reason, it was a goal that, over the years, just seems to get better and better.'

(Yes - in case you hadn't spotted it, the big defender was one Alan Hansen, while the striker was a certain Gary Lineker. If there was one goal the two were certainly never going to agree on, this was it. For the record, Liverpool won the Final 3-1).

Hansen v Lineker
MOTD

The Goal They Agree On

Both Alan and Gary put Maradona's mesmeric second against England, in the World Cup quarter-final of 1986, on their lists of the best goals they've seen. It was a dazzling solo run that would make virtually everyone's top three, and many judge it to be the finest goal ever scored.

Still in his own half when he took possession, Maradona spun and swerved away from the English midfield, then set off towards goal, gathering pace all the time. On a poor surface, which made the ball kick and bobble in front of him, he still managed to keep control as he dribbled past defender after defender. In the penalty area, falling after one final desperate tackle from Terry Butcher, he still managed to slide the ball past the advancing Peter Shilton. Pure genius – unfortunately for England!

● **Maradona weaves through the English defence to score Argentina's 2nd goal.**

FOR the past four years MOTD magazine has included with its October issues an excellent poster, featuring the 100 best players in Britain. Voted for by the cream of the country's pundits and managers, it's essential reading …

Now MOTD Annual takes this great idea one step further with a roll of honour that presents the top 100 footballers from the years 1964 through to the present day. The rules were extremely simple … to be considered the football personnel must have played in English League football at any time between the season when MOTD was first seen on the TV screens through to the present day. Important factors taken into consideration were, of course, soccer talent, position played and also the number of games played and time spent in the English game.

We make no apologies for sparking off arguments on who finished where and who did and didn't make it onto this definitive of lists … but it's refreshing to see that the top five players are all British stars.

100 ANDREI KANCHELSKIS

Flying winger from the Ukraine with blistering acceleration and audacious skill on the ball. He played in both England and Scotland.

99 RAY WILKINS

Smooth and intelligent English midfield operator whose style of play was almost continental.

98 ARCHIE GEMMILL

Workaholic Scottish midfield man who was also highly skilful on the ball.

97 JOHNNY BYRNE

England and West Ham forward known for his vision and tremendous passing skills. Johnny played football with a smile on his face.

96 MATTHEW LE TISSIER

Supremely gifted forward, magical on the ball and has scored some of the Premiership's finest goals.

95 RAY CLEMENCE

Terrifically agile 'keeper, for a long time rated Shilton's equal, meaning that they alternated in goal for England.

94 CELESTINE BABAYARO

Versatile and athletic left-sided defender from Nigeria.

93 KENNY SANSOM

Consistent high-level performer at full-back.

92 NEVILLE SOUTHALL

Winner of a record 92 caps for Wales, a terrific 'keeper who played in the Premiership last season, aged 41.

91 ALAN MULLERY

Competitive and energetic midfield player and a scorer of some spectacular goals.

90 VIV ANDERSON

Tall, leggy, athletic full-back, always eager to break forward (when he often notched a vital goal).

89 STEVE HEIGHWAY

Tricky wide player who was also a smart finisher, he now runs Liverpool's impressively productive youth development scheme.

88 ROGER HUNT

Deceptively talented Liverpool and England goal-machine, the Rush or Fowler of his day (only he's the one with the World Cup winner's medal!).

87 KANU

Giant Nigerian striker, full of tricks, flicks and leggy dribbles, with fantastic ball control for a such a big man.

86 JOHN BARNES

Beautifully balanced, devastating left-winger who re-thought his game when running short of pace in later years to become an extremely effective midfield playmaker.

85 SOL CAMPBELL

Quick, strong and powerful centre-back, approaching his prime and approaching world class.

84 EMLYN HUGHES

Always competitive and determined, switching to defence from midfield made this former captain of England, Liverpool and A Question of Sport, even better.

83 STUART PEARCE

Uncompromising left-back and a fearsome dead ball striker, he was brave enough to take a shoot-out spot-kick in Euro 96, having missed in similar circumstances at the World Cup of 1990.

82 COLIN TODD

Cool, composed centre-back with a very keen footballing brain, which he's since put to good use in football management.

81 MARK HUGHES

Fiercely competitive Welsh striker, now managing the national side, noted for netting some amazing volleys at the height of his playing powers.

80 RODNEY MARSH

Stylish and flamboyant entertainer with the ball at his feet, who was a joy to watch yet must have been a nightmare to manage.

79 NOBBY STILES

In many ways the Paul Ince of his day, Nobby was an effective enforcer in the middle of the pitch in the 1960s and good enough to win a World Cup winner's medal.

78 PAUL INCE

The self-styled 'guv'nor', a midfield anchorman renowned for his competitive attitude, strong tackling and bringing a never-say-die spirit to the game.

77 TERRY BUTCHER

Stalwart stopper at the heart of England's defence for 10 years, he shed blood for the cause on more than one occasion.

76 PAOLO DI CANIO

Mercurial Italian striker, wonderfully talented but with a suspect temperament.

75 FRANK McLINTOCK

Strong and resolute international defender from north of the border.

74 PATRICK VIEIRA

Powerful, athletic midfielder – another of France's current top performers.

73 CHRIS WADDLE

Classy, seemingly very laid-back English wide player with a magical touch on the ball.

72 CHARLIE COOKE

Entertaining Scottish international winger who loved to dribble and take players on.

71 MARK LAWRENSON

Quick, athletic centre-back, strong in the tackle, yet elegant and controlled with the ball at his feet.

70 JACK CHARLTON

Giraffe-like centre-half at the heart of England's World Cup winning side, became a living legend when he managed the Republic of Ireland.

69 ARNOLD MUHREN

Dutch midfielder with great vision who was able to puncture defences with telling passes from his superb left foot.

68 STEVE McMANAMAN

Dangerous dribbler with wonderful ball control, he's taking his game to a higher level after winning the European Cup in his first season with Real Madrid.

67 DAVID PLATT

Energetic central midfielder with a great knack for timing his arrival in the penalty box to score vital goals.

66 JAAP STAM

Awesome, man-mountain of a central defender, dominant in the air and a tough tackler on the ground.

65 STEVE COPPELL

Exciting and classy wide midfielder, an intelligent user of the ball.

64 MICHAEL OWEN

Sprinter-paced striker hit by hamstring injuries which have dented his progress. But still potentially a world great.

63 GORDON STRACHAN

Once football's Peter Pan, often the best player on the park when still performing in midfield in his late thirties, he's now set his astute soccer brain to management.

62 PAUL GASCOIGNE

Flawed genius, probably the most talented Englishman of his generation. Yet injuries – some self-inflicted – have robbed him of true greatness.

61 DAVID SEAMAN

England's best goalkeeper of the last decade, noted for some brilliant penalty saves.

60 PAUL McGRATH

Rock solid Republic of Ireland defender, his commitment was such that he played with damaged knees when scarcely able to train.

59 HARRY KEWELL

Australian with a devastating left foot, a swag-bag full of talent, and an eye for scoring some spectacular goals.

58 BRIAN LAUDRUP

Stylish wide player from Denmark, his tremendous control on long, incisive runs makes him difficult to stop.

57 KEVIN HECTOR

A clever, nippy finisher who scored goals despite lacking any great physical presence.

56 GEORGE WEAH

Outstandingly talented striker with great movement and technique, and a former World Footballer of the Year.

55 THIERRY HENRY

Another from the current powerful squad of Frenchmen, he is lightning-fast and has a devastating eye for goal.

54 DAVID NISH

Composed, assured full-back capable of breaking forward to productive effect.

53 JUNINHO

Built more like a jockey than a footballer, this tiny Brazilian forward with wonderful ball skills is a thrilling sight when he sets off on his electrifying, darting runs.

52 IAN WRIGHT

A late starter in football, he still became Arsenal's record goalscorer, using his great pace and natural finishing talent to turn the ball into the net.

51 MARTIN PETERS

Rangy midfielder who broke cleverly from that area of the pitch to score many vital goals for his clubs and for England.

50 GIANFRANCO ZOLA

Hugely popular with Chelsea fans, the Italian ace has wonderful skills on the ball.

49 JOHNNY GILES

One of the Republic of Ireland's greatest players, a classy midfielder who always used the ball well.

48 DWIGHT YORKE

Trinidad and Tobago's silkily skilled striker who has made himself at home in the Premiership.

47 NORMAN HUNTER

Fearsome centre-back, as tough a tackler as there's ever been.

46 JIMMY ARMFIELD

Neat and tidy England full-back, now a respected Radio 5 Live football reporter.

45 TERRY PAINE

Winger turned midfielder who made more than 800 League appearances.

44 JIMMY McILROY

Burnley's favourite son - an inside-forward of the 50s and 60s who had sheer artistry in his boots.

43 CLIFF JONES

Spurs and Welsh flying winger who was a speed merchant with brilliant ball control.

42 GRAEME SOUNESS

Committed midfielder with great passing skills and a devastating shot, but an intimidating tackler, too.

41 DAVE MACKAY

Rock-like Scottish defender, tenacious in the tackle and no slouch on the ball, either.

40 TONY ADAMS

A giant in terms of performance and personality, a defensive lynchpin for club and country.

39 ALLAN CLARKE

Deceptively slight-looking goalscorer, and very effective rather than spectacular.

38 PETER OSGOOD

Tall and well-balanced striker with a great touch on the ball, given his size.

37 OSVALDO ARDILES

Argentina's clever and gifted operator in the middle of the park.

36 LOU MACARI

Neat, nimble and tricky Scottish international midfielder.

35 PAT JENNINGS

Northern Ireland's best-ever 'keeper, very agile for his size, and famous for having the biggest hands in football.

34 IAN RUSH

Fantastic, instinctive finisher, he had great speed and was always willing to defend from the front by closing down opponents.

33 TREVOR FRANCIS

The first player to be transferred for £1 million in this country, he possessed electric pace and excellent technique.

32 ALAN SHEARER

Strong, powerful centre-forward, one of the finest goalscorers of the last decade.

31 TREVOR BROOKING

Classy and elegant midfield creator, and a genuinely two-footed player.

30 ALAN BALL

Non-stop, hustling, bustling mini-midfield marvel.

29 PETER SHILTON

Running Banks close for the title of England's best 'keeper, he holds the record for the most England appearances at 125.

28 MARCEL DESAILLY

Another of France's top stars, a quick, strong defender and very comfortable on the ball.

27 EMMANUEL PETIT

Energetic midfielder from the current outstanding generation of French footballers.

26 GLENN HODDLE

Fabulously talented playmaker who excelled in delivering long, exquisite passes.

25 PETER SCHMEICHEL

One of the greatest goalkeepers - arguably, the greatest - the game has ever seen.

24 ALAN HANSEN

Majestic centre-half, the finest defender ever to come out of Scotland.

23 BILLY BREMNER

Tough, combative, yet skilful, pint-sized Scottish midfield terrier.

22 KEVIN KEEGAN

England's current manager was a lively, determined, tricky striker who continually worked and worked at his game, eventually twice becoming European Footballer of the Year.

21 RYAN GIGGS

Outstanding left-sided winger, possessing dazzling dribbling skills and electric pace.

20 GEOFF HURST

Top class finisher, still the only player ever to score a hat-trick in the World Cup Final.

19 GARY LINEKER

England's second-highest goalscorer and a lethally quick penalty-box finisher.

18 LIAM BRADY

Known as 'Chippy', an exceptional Republic of Ireland international with a great left peg who also enjoyed seven great years playing in Italy.

17 ROY KEANE

Currently the best midfield player in the country, an awesomely competitive, dynamic footballer who is loved by the Old Trafford supporters.

16 JIM BAXTER

Highly-gifted and artful Scottish ball-player, his finest moment came at Wembley when the Auld Enemy beat the new World Champions 3-2 in 1967.

15 JOHN TOSHACK

An astute goalscorer from Wales who has gone on to manage the mighty Real Madrid.

14 DENNIS BERGKAMP

Arsenal's Dutch master, a striker possessing wonderful talent and technique.

13 DENIS LAW

Tremendous Scottish goalscorer, a quick-silver finisher in the penalty box.

12 GORDON BANKS

England's best ever 'keeper, and a World Cup winner, his career was cut short after an eye injury.

Top 100 Footballers

11 JOHN CHARLES

The greatest Welsh footballer ever, he's worshipped at Juventus for scoring 93 goals in 155 games for them between 1957 and 1962.

10 BRYAN ROBSON

Few midfielders have come close to matching him for competitiveness and courage. Manchester United and England's Captain Marvel for many years, he picked up countless injuries during his career but always returned to his team's engine room as committed and determined as ever. In his prime, his energy, drive and eye for goal marked him out as world class.

9 JIMMY GREAVES

A remarkable goalscorer, and a scorer of some remarkable goals. No great worker on the pitch, and no great trainer off it, he was nevertheless quite deadly in front of goal. A player who loved to entertain the crowd, his 44 goals from just 57 England appearances shows how effective he was at hitting the target at the highest level.

8 DAVID BECKHAM

At just 25, he stands on the verge of greatness. He possesses the best right foot in the country, possibly in Europe, and combines it with fantastic stamina and a highly competitive winner's attitude. He can be used out wide on the right, from where his peerless crossing is deadly, or in a central midfield position, unlocking defences with his sublime passing skills.

7 ERIC CANTONA

Wayward genius who found his stage at Old Trafford and galvanised Manchester United into becoming the team of the last decade. A Gallic cocktail of flicks, touches, glorious passing and devastating finishing, all topped by a dash of arrogance that almost destroyed his career. He continually practised and worked on his game almost to the day he stopped playing altogether.

6 RUUD GULLIT

Majestic Dutch total footballer who began as a striker but later, particularly at Chelsea, moved back to midfield and even defence. A powerfully built player, equally commanding in the air or on the ground, this gifted player possessed marvellous technique and certainly wasn't flattered when voted both European and World Footballer of the Year in 1987.

5 KENNY DALGLISH

Scotland's greatest ever player holds his country's record for the number of caps won and goals scored. A striker blessed with stunning ball skills and the sharpest of soccer brains, he was a tremendous team-player, not just an individualist. Since retiring from playing, he has also gone on to manage Championship-winning sides at Liverpool and Blackburn.

4 STANLEY MATTHEWS

A wonderfully skilful winger known as the Wizard of Dribble, he turned full-backs inside out with magical trickery and devastating acceleration. He produced such a virtuoso performance in the 1953 FA Cup Final that, even though team-mate Stan Mortensen scored a hat-trick, it is known as The Matthews Final. Incredibly, he kept playing until he was 50!

3 BOBBY CHARLTON

England's top goalscorer was a sublimely talented striker who later switched to midfield. He was famous for his thunderbolt shot and his impeccable conduct on and off the field. A vital player in England's World Cup win, and Manchester United's European Cup triumph in 1968, he is now one of football's finest ambassadors.

2 BOBBY MOORE

Pele said of him: "The greatest defender I have ever faced," which says it all. England's most-capped outfield player, he captained that famous World Cup winning side in 1966. Not particularly pacey or strong in the air, he more than compensated with superb timing and masterly reading of the game. He died depressingly young, at just 51.

1 GEORGE BEST

The finest player of his generation, very probably the best Britain has ever produced. Simply a genius with the ball at his feet, possessing limitless skills to outwit even the finest defenders in the game. European Footballer of the Year in 1968, he played 37 times for Northern Ireland but never in the final stages of the World Cup or European Championships. Had he done so, he might be held in even higher regard than he is today.

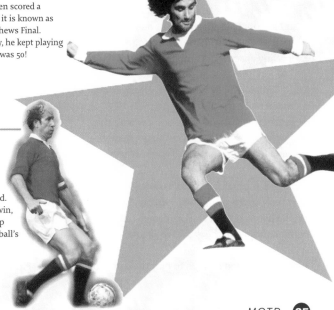

Short of being a superstar Premiership player, the next-best career in professional football would seem to be as a commentator on the game. One of the best in the business is Match of the Day's Tony Gubba and here he explains what you see on your TV screens through the eyes and voice of ... **THE MAN WITH THE MIKE**

SO you want to be a television football commentator on Match of the Day! Well, don't be surprised or disheartened, but you're not alone.

Almost every week the commentary team of John Motson, Barry Davies, Jon Champion and myself receive letters from young viewers expressing exactly that ambition.

These letters usually begin with effusive comments like "it's the best programme on TV," or "I never miss it," and almost inevitably they end with the same question: "Can you advise me how to become a football commentator?"

Kicking a football as a professional player is obviously every young boy's dream, but high on the list of second choices comes the job of commentating on the game we all love.

If you're not good enough to play the game for a living, then where better to be at three o'clock on a Saturday afternoon than perched on a television gantry, describing the action and excitement, broadcasting your opinions to an armchair audience that may total 10 million people or more?

It's not just boys who want to get into the commentary box. Girls, too, write in with similar enquiries.

When one of the commentators sits down in the Match of the Day office, on the 5th floor of Television Centre, to write a reply to a letter like those I've described, that 'how do I become a soccer commentator?' question can really have us scratching our heads.

Sorry if it's disappointing, but there isn't a set route or simple formula that you can advise someone to follow.

Getting a job as a television football commentator can sometimes be more the result of good luck than good planning, more accident than design.

Being the right person, in the right place, at the right time, is a knack that's impossible to teach, but you can help your cause by being thoroughly prepared to grasp the opportunity, if it arises.

Obviously, you need to be dedicated and determined, with a burning ambition to become a commentator in the first place, believing whole-heartedly that it's the only job for you.

Even more importantly, you'll have to have the basic talent to do the job: a good broadcasting voice, the confidence to describe what you see without embarrassment, a thorough knowledge and understanding of the game and its laws, and the ability to instantly identify literally hundreds of players without waiting for a glimpse of the number or name on the backs of their shirts.

With all the football that's now shown on the various television channels, like the BBC, ITV, Sky Sports, Channel's Four & Five etc., there are obviously more football commentators around than ever before. But that's still only about a dozen in total!

If there's one word that summarises the most important stepping-stone on the road to becoming a football commentator, that word is ... journalism.

Man with the Mike

Since Match of the Day began in the 1960s, all the commentators who've appeared on the programme have been ex-journalists – people who began their working lives as reporters on provincial and national newspapers, or local radio stations, before making the move into television journalism and eventually on to Match of the Day.

Football is unique among all major sports shown on British television because not one of the game's commentators was ever a professional player.

Unlike in rugby, cricket, tennis and other professional sports, no ex-footballer has yet made the transition from playing the game to holding the commentary microphone.

Don't be confused by the former England and West Ham player Trevor Brooking, and others like him, who sometimes work as a co-commentator on a live match, adding their valued opinions to a commentary being done by someone else; or former Scotland and Liverpool defender Alan Hansen who works as

a studio expert, or pundit, analysing the action over slow-motion replays; or Gary Lineker, who scored goals for England, Leicester, Everton, Barcelona and Spurs, and who has now replaced Des Lynam as Match of the Day's front man.

None of them do the main football commentary, calling the action as it happens, identifying the players and broadcasting for the whole 90 minutes of a game, even if only a twenty-five minute edited package is shown on the programme that night.

In American sports broadcasting they have a role called the 'colour' commentator and that's about as far as our ex-pros have got.

So if you want to be a Match of the Day football commentator, don't think a career as a player will guarantee it, think journalism!

A look into the backgrounds and careers of the current commentary team should prove the point.

John Motson, the son of a Methodist minister, started as a junior reporter on the Barnet Press, moving to the Sheffield Telegraph, then BBC Radio Sheffield, before joining network Radio 2 to commentate on football, boxing and tennis.

It was after Kenneth Wolstenholme – 'they think it's all over, it is now' – left the BBC in 1971 that John joined Match of the Day and his first game was the classic FA Cup tie between Hereford and Newcastle United.

Barry Davies got his first broadcasting experience with the British Forces Network in Cologne, Germany, later joining BBC Radio and becoming a football correspondent with The Times.

Jon Champion cut his teeth as a football commentator with BBC Radio Leeds and later Radio 5 Live.

My own background is similar. I was a cub reporter on the Sale & Stretford Guardian, moving on to the Blackburn Evening Telegraph, the Daily Mirror, then Southern Television in Southampton.

I was later the BBC's north-west of England correspondent based in Liverpool and joined the television sports department in the early 70s as a presenter of Sportsnight and Grandstand. My first commentaries were on table tennis, then cycling, skating and eventually football.

Of course, there is one thing that all the Match of the Day commentators have in common, and that's an absolute passion for the game of football. Although none of us were talented enough to become professionals, we all played as enthusiastic amateurs. Indeed, until a few years ago, myself, John Motson, Martin Tyler and Alan Parry would all turn out regularly for a Commentators XI.

So, to summarise, if you want to be a television football commentator: play the game to as high a standard as you can, study professional football, its teams, its players, and its history as if swotting for an exam, and try to secure a first foot-hold on the ladder to your dreams by getting a job as a trainee reporter on your local newspaper or radio station.

Then, who knows, in ten years' time you may be commentating on Match of the Day as Michael Owen scores his 250th goal for Liverpool, or as Doncaster Rovers beat Manchester United 4-0 to win the Premiership title at Old Trafford.

Life is more fun when you have dreams.

Barry Davies

Top Ten Musts

Good Luck
Dedication
Determination
Good Speaking Voice
Confidence
No Embarrassment
Know the Laws of the Game
Able to Identify Players
Play the Game
Journalistic Know-how

Top TV Team Squad Line-Up?

Top TV Team Squad Line-Up?

Bob Wilson
Mark Lawrenson
Alan Hansen
Tony Gubba
Alan Parry
Gary Lineker
Trevor Brooking
Mark Bright
Jon Champion
John Motson
Andy Gray
Trevor Francis
Martin Tyler

Can you name the famous player from the following picture clues of items found in his theatre dressing-room, and the football theatres where he performed?

A North-easterner, born in 1961, this player enjoyed a glittering career at club and international level. He finally hung up his boots in 1999, but having always been an entertaining player he has since trod the stage in pantomime.

His first club was Carlisle United, his last Hartlepool United. In between, he played for some of the most famous clubs in the land, and developed a fondness for chocolate bars. He still has that – those sweets in his dressing-room weren't there to be thrown to the audience.

In the panto he dons a crown, but during his career he picked up 59 England caps. He was still serving his country last summer, too, having been part of Kevin Keegan's training staff for Euro 2000.

The production he was starring in was Sleeping Beauty, playing the part of King Pedro of Gallowgate. On the pitch, playing as a strike-partner to MOTD's Gary Lineker, he formed one of the finest front pairings England has ever had. With the pair in tandem, England reached the World Cup quarter-finals in 1986 and the semi-finals four years later.

During his career, he was able to call some of football's finest stages 'home' Park. If anything he was appreciated even more during his two spells at St James' Park in Newcastle.

▲ PETER BEARDSLEY

There have been 30 Goal of the Season awards since MOTD began the famous competition back in the early 1970s. But which of those brilliant belters is the best? We've set ourselves the near impossible task of finding the

GOAL OF THE GOAL OF THE SEASON

ONLY one player has achieved it twice. Only once has it been a header. It's been scored against Arsenal five times, Liverpool five times - and Israel once. Two brothers have scored it, as has a non-league player, but not the likes of Alan Shearer, Ian Rush, Gary Lineker or Eric Cantona. It's the Goal Of The Season, the ultimate annual accolade for football's most breathtaking strikes.

But is it possible to judge which is the best of the best, to decide which great goal is, in fact, the greatest? Over the next few pages, we've described each goal and graded it in the following categories:

Genius – a mark of a goal's invention and originality (from 1 to 10)
Skill level – a measure of the degree of difficulty involved (from 1 to 10)
Action – whether a goal came from a free kick (7), or open play (10)
Dodgy defending – a negative score, depending on opposition errors (from 5 to 0)
Net bulge – an indication of the goal's spectacle and impact (from 1 to 10)
The scores add up to give an overall rating. Is the goal with the highest rating the best that's ever been showcased on MOTD? Check out the scores and see what you think ...

THE GOAL ROLL OF HONOUR

1971 - ERNIE HUNT, Coventry
1972 - RONNIE RADFORD, Hereford
1973 - PETER OSGOOD, Chelsea
1974 - ALAN MULLERY, Fulham
1975 - MICKEY WALSH, Blackpool
1976 - GERRY FRANCIS, QPR
1977 - TERRY McDERMOTT, Liverpool
1978 - ARCHIE GEMMILL, Nott'm Forest
1979 - RAY KENNEDY, Liverpool
1980 - JUSTIN FASHANU, Norwich
1981 - TONY MORLEY, Aston Villa
1982 - CYRILLE REGIS, WBA
1983 - KENNY DALGLISH, Scotland
1984 - DANNY WALLACE, Southampton
1985 - GRAEME SHARP, Everton
1986 - BRYAN ROBSON, England
1987 - KEITH HOUCHEN, Coventry

1988 - JOHN ALDRIDGE, Liverpool
1989 - JOHN ALDRIDGE, Liverpool
1990 - IAN WRIGHT, Crystal Palace
1991 - PAUL GASCOIGNE, Tottenham
1992 - MICKEY THOMAS, Wrexham/
MICHAEL THOMAS, Liverpool
1993 - DALIAN ATKINSON, Aston Villa
1994 - ROD WALLACE, Leeds
1995 - MATT LE TISSIER, Southampton
1996 - TONY YEBOAH, Leeds
1997 - TREVOR SINCLAIR, QPR
1998 - DENNIS BERGKAMP, Arsenal
1999 - RYAN GIGGS, Man United
2000 - PAOLO DI CANIO, West Ham United

THE GOALS IN DETAIL

1971 - ERNIE HUNT for Coventry v Everton, League Div 1, Oct 1970
Hunt crashes home a volley after team-mate Willie Carr tees up a free kick for him with a 'donkey' kick – jumping up with the ball between his heels, then releasing it in mid-air. (This was later ruled illegal contact at a free kick, and banned).

Genius 10 / Skill level 8 / Action - free kick 7 / Dodgy defending 0 / Net bulge 9

RATING: 34

1972 - RONNIE RADFORD for Hereford v Newcastle, FA Cup, Feb 1972
A thunderous shot from distance which levelled the scores and set up the famous Cup upset for the non-league side.

Genius 7 / Skill level 7 / Action - open play 10 / Dodgy defending -1 / Net bulge 10

RATING: 33

1973 - PETER OSGOOD for Chelsea v Arsenal, FA Cup, March 1973
Latching onto a high ricochet, Osgood smashes home a left foot volley from the edge of the penalty area, leaving Arsenal 'keeper Bob Wilson no chance.

Genius 6 / Skill level 8 / Action - open play 10 / Dodgy defending -1 / Net bulge 6

RATING: 29

1974 - ALAN MULLERY for Fulham v Leicester, FA Cup, Jan 1974
Meeting a knee-high crossfield ball in his stride, the Fulham man strikes it full on the volley to lash the ball into the top corner of the net.

Genius 7 / Skill level 7 / Action - open play 10 / Dodgy defending 0 / Net bulge 8

RATING: 32

1975 - MICKEY WALSH for Blackpool v Sunderland, League Div 2, Feb 1975
A run from the half-way line followed by a check and spin inside, ending with a missile of a left foot shot from the edge of the penalty area, crashing in off the far post.

Genius 8 / Skill level 8 / Action - open play 10 / Dodgy defending -1 / Net bulge 9

RATING: 34

1976 - GERRY FRANCIS for QPR v Liverpool, League Div 1, Aug 1975
An incisive move down the middle of the pitch involving Stan Bowles and Don Givens cuts the Liverpool back line apart, and Francis gallops through to slide a precise finish past Ray Clemence.

Genius 8 / Skill level 7 / Action - open play 10 / Dodgy defending -1 / Net bulge 7

RATING: 31

of the Season

1977 - **TERRY McDERMOTT for Liverpool v Everton, FA Cup, April 1977**
Outside the opposition penalty area, McDermott cuts inside a defender before placing an exquisite chip over the stranded Everton 'keeper.

Genius 8 / Skill level 8 / Action - open play 10 / Dodgy defending -2 / Net bulge 8

RATING: 32

1978 - **ARCHIE GEMMILL for Nott'm Forest v Arsenal, League Div 1, Jan 1978**
Gemmill breaks up an Arsenal move, feeds Withe, then races upfield to meet his team-mate's cross and sweep the ball home.

Genius 7 / Skill level 7 / Action - open play 10 / Dodgy defending -2 / Net bulge 7

RATING: 29

1979 - **RAY KENNEDY for Liverpool v Derby, League Div 1, Feb 1979**

A drilled crossfield ball is met by Kennedy bursting forward. Clever control and footwork takes him beyond the defence and around the 'keeper for a simple tap in.

Genius 7 / Skill level 8 / Action - open play 10 / Dodgy defending -2 / Net bulge 7

RATING: 30

1980 - **JUSTIN FASHANU for Norwich v Liverpool, League Div 1, Feb 1980**
On the corner of Liverpool's box, a first touch flick-up turns Fashanu back inside and a second touch, fiercely hit volley flies over Alan Hansen into the far top corner.

Genius 8 / Skill level 8 / Action - open play 10 / Dodgy defending -1 / Net bulge 9

RATING: 34

1981 - **TONY MORLEY for Aston Villa v Everton, League Div 1, Feb 1981**
Given the ball just inside the Everton half, Morley advances at pace and from just outside the box he crashes home a ferocious shot.

Genius 7 / Skill level 7 / Action - open play 10 / Dodgy defending -1 / Net bulge 8

RATING: 31

1982 - **CYRILLE REGIS for WBA v Norwich, FA Cup, Feb 1982**
Clever chest control and turn allows the West Brom centre forward to accelerate towards the box before unleashing a powerful, unstoppable shot from distance.

Genius 8 / Skill level 7 / Action - open play 10 / Dodgy defending -1 / Net bulge 8

RATING: 32

1983 - **KENNY DALGLISH for Scotland v Belgium, Euro '84 qualifier, Dec 1982**
Fantastic right foot control and turn takes Dalglish around one defender and into the box. Side-stepping a second defender, he fires a rising shot home with his left foot.

Genius 8 / Skill level 9 / Action - open play 10 / Dodgy defending -2 / Net bulge 9

RATING: 34

1984 - **DANNY WALLACE for Southampton v Liverpool, League Div 1, March 1984**

Wallace reacts lightning-fast to a far-post headed knock-down, hooking the ball into the net from close range with an athletic overhead kick.

Genius 8 / Skill level 8 / Action - open play 10 / Dodgy defending -1 / Net bulge 8

RATING: 33

1985 - **GRAEME SHARP for Everton v Liverpool, League Div 1, Oct 1984**
A first touch takes Sharp right, away from his marker, while his second – a searing volley from distance back across to the left – rockets into the net.

Genius 8 / Skill level 8 / Action - open play 10/ Dodgy defending -2 / Net bulge 8

RATING: 32

1986 - **BRYAN ROBSON for England v Israel, friendly International, Feb 1986**
Picked out by a pinpoint ball into the box from Hoddle, as he steals unmarked into the box, Robson sweeps a beautifully timed volley into the top corner of the net.

Genius 7 / Skill level 8 / Action -open play 10 / Dodgy defending -1 / Net bulge 8

RATING: 32

1987 - KEITH HOUCHEN for Coventry v Tottenham, FA Cup, May 1987

Feeding Dave Bennett out on the right, Houchen spins away into the box. When the cross comes in, he flings himself forward and scores with a dramatic diving header.

Genius 7 / Skill level 7 / Action - open play 10 / Dodgy defending 0 / Net bulge 9

RATING: 33

1988 - JOHN ALDRIDGE for Liverpool v Nott'm Forest, FA Cup, April 1988

Liverpool build a move down Forest's left and John Barnes sends in a teasing cross which the in-rushing Aldridge meets full on the volley to thump home.

Genius 7 / Skill level 7 / Action - open play 10 / Dodgy defending -1 / Net bulge 9

RATING: 32

1989 - JOHN ALDRIDGE for Liverpool v Everton, FA Cup, May 1989

Breaking quickly, a long ball from defence is clipped inside by Steve McMahon for Aldridge to place high inside the post from the edge of the box.

Genius 6 / Skill level 7 / Action - open play 10 / Dodgy defending -1 / Net bulge 8

RATING: 30

1990 - IAN WRIGHT for Crystal Palace v Man United, FA Cup, May 1990

On as a substitute, Wright's first contribution is to beat one defender to a through ball, cut inside a second, and drive a low shot beyond United's diving 'keeper.

Genius 7 / Skill level 8 / Action - open play 10 / Dodgy defending -2 / Net bulge 8

RATING: 31

1991 - PAUL GASCOIGNE for Tottenham v Arsenal, FA Cup, April 1991

Gascoigne cracks a central free kick from fully 30 yards away from goal with such power and curl that David Seaman in the Arsenal goal cannot keep it out.

Genius 9 / Skill level 8 / Action - free kick 7 / Dodgy defending 0 / Net bulge 9

RATING: 33

1992 - MICKEY THOMAS for Wrexham v Arsenal, FA Cup, Jan 1992, and MICHAEL THOMAS for Liverpool v Sunderland, FA Cup, May 1992

Another scorching free kick beats the helpless Seaman when veteran Thomas thrashes the ball with great power beyond his reach from the corner of the box.

Genius 7 / Skill level 8 / Action - free kick 7 / Dodgy defending 0 / Net bulge 8

RATING: 30

An equally marvellous goal comes from namesake Michael, who latches onto a chipped ball into the box to hook home with a volley hit on the turn.

Genius 7 / Skill level 7 / Action - open play 10 / Dodgy defending -2 / Net bulge 8

RATING: 30

1993 - DALIAN ATKINSON for Aston Villa v Wimbledon, Prem League, Oct 1992

Collecting the ball midway in his own half, Atkinson sets off and beats defender after defender before finding the perfect chip from outside the box over a stranded 'keeper.

Genius 9 / Skill level 9 / Action - open play 10 / Dodgy defending -1 / Net bulge 9

RATING: 36

1994 - ROD WALLACE for Leeds v Tottenham, Prem League, April 1994

The brother of the 1984 winner collects the ball in his own half, sets off on a mazy run taking him out to the touch-line, past three defenders, and on into the box where he curls a lovely shot inside the far post.

Genius 9 / Skill level 9 / Action - open play 10 / Dodgy defending -2 / Net bulge 8

RATING: 34

of the Season

MOTD

1995 - MATT LE TISSIER for Southampton v Blackburn, Prem League, Dec 1994

A meandering dribble takes Le Tissier into space midway into Blackburn's half, from where he strikes an astonishing shot which dips into the top corner of the net.

Genius 9 / Skill level 10 / Action - open play 10 / Dodgy defending -2 / Net bulge 8

RATING: 35

1996 - TONY YEBOAH for Leeds v Liverpool, Prem League, Aug 1995

Taking possession a long way outside Liverpool's box, Yeboah lets fly with a ferocious drive which rockets into the goal off the underside of the crossbar.

Genius 7 / Skill level 8 / Action - open play 10 / Dodgy defending -1 / Net bulge 8

RATING: 32

1997 - TREVOR SINCLAIR for QPR v Barnsley, FA Cup, Feb 1997

Sinclair, readjusting to a cross played slightly behind him, launches himself into the air outside Barnsley's box to connect with a startling overhead volley which arrows into the net.

Genius 9 / Skill level 10 / Action - open play 10 / Dodgy defending -1 Net bulge 9

RATING: 37

1998 - DENNIS BERGKAMP for Arsenal v Leicester, Prem League, Aug 1997

Chasing a ball into the opposition box, Bergkamp takes the pace off it with one touch, then ball juggles past a defender to tee himself up for a silky side-footed strike.

Genius 9 / Skill level 9 / Action - open play 10 / Dodgy defending -1 / Net bulge 9

RATING: 36

1999 - RYAN GIGGS for Man United v Arsenal, FA Cup, April 1999

Astonishing solo run from the Welsh wideman, sprinting from within his own half into the opposition penalty area and crashing home a rising shot from a tight angle.

Genius 10 / Skill level 10 / Action - open play 10 / Dodgy defending -2 / Net bulge 10

RATING: 38

2000 - PAOLO DI CANIO for West Ham United v Wimbledon, Prem League, March 2000

Meeting a deep cross into the box, Di Canio strikes a wonderfully controlled volley with the outside of his foot into the goal's far corner.

Genius 10 / Skill level 9 / Action - open play 10 / Dodgy defending -1 Net bulge 9

RATING: 37

So Giggs' effort in '99, by a whisker from Sinclair and Di Canio, is the Goal Of The Goal Of The Season. The best goal ever showcased on MOTD ..? Perhaps, but only so far ...

Roy of the Rovers

A brief look at the life and times of football's definitive hero, serving as a scene-setting prelude to the following, momentous, new story.

ROY Race, the greatest player of his or any other generation, burst onto the football scene as a raw but prodigiously talented teenager. Tall, strong and powerfully-built, he was classic centre-forward material. Yet he was no mere battering ram blunt instrument, for Melchester's favourite son possessed terrific skills and a fantastic footballing brain.

Early in his career, Roy formed a devastating striking partnership with life-long friend Blackie Gray. Within two years of their debut for Rovers, the pair had won Championship medals. Countless other honours followed as – apart from occasional sticky patches – the club dominated both domestically and in Europe, with Roy plundering goal after goal with his trademark 'rocket' left foot shot.

Away from football, marriage to Penny and three children (twins Melinda and Roy junior, known to all as Rocky and youngest daughter Diana -) gave Roy a settled family life.

Eventually, the quintessential number nine took on the role of player-manager at Rovers. Yet when the side seemed stronger than ever, poised to pull off a Premiership title and Champions League 'double', a fateful helicopter crash left Roy so badly injured he could never play again.

Recovery was slow. Penny feared bouts of drinking and depression would destroy her husband, but she was powerless to prevent them. Then in Italy, in circumstances which remain a mystery to this day, Penny was killed in a car crash. Roy had hit rock bottom.

Meanwhile Blackie took charge at Rovers, and though young Rocky had forced his way into the first team, for many the Melchester Magic had gone. Top players quit the club; a slide down the League ensued. Most shocking of all, a bribery scandal involving a director shook the club and football to its foundations. Blackie and the board resigned. Relegation followed. In freefall, Rovers spiraled towards rock bottom, too.

But at this darkest hour, the club's talisman returned. Forming an alliance with the unsavory Vinter Brothers, who had their own agenda for getting involved, Roy became co-owner of Rovers. He installed his daughter Melinda as Managing Director, while he took charge of team affairs. The legend's mere presence lifted the club. Brilliant transfer dealings, inspired coaching and bold tactics brought promotion back to the Premiership, followed last season by a startling Championship triumph. This feat was all the more remarkable, as it was achieved against a backdrop of boardroom battles.

With the troublesome Vinters proving a constant drain on the club's resources, Mel and Roy have now embarked upon an audacious and dangerous scheme to oust them. They have bought off the pair with Mel Park, Rovers' historic home ground, planning to relocate the club to a yet-to-be-built new stadium and entertainment complex.

It is the most daring gamble Roy Race has ever taken ...

... "BY WEDNESDAY MORNING."

SORRY, ROY – JEFF'S NOWHERE NEAR READY.

PETE'S A GOOD 'KEEPER, BOSS...

I KNOW, JEFF – HE'S JUST BEEN UNLUCKY. BUT WE CAN'T AFFORD FOR HIM TO BE UNLUCKY AGAIN ..!

ROY AND HIS NUMBER TWO, GEOFF GILES, WANDERED OUT ON TO THE MEL PARK PITCH...

CAN'T HELP THINKING IT'D BE BETTER IF THE PLAYERS DIDN'T KNOW HOW VITAL THIS SECOND PHASE CHAMPIONS LEAGUE MONEY IS.

CAN'T TURN THE CLOCK BACK, GEOFF. COULD HARDLY KEEP THEM THE DARK ABOUT SELLING TH HOME GROUND ANYWAY!

I'M STILL STAGGERED YOU'VE DONE IT! ROY RACE, SELLING MEL PARK... ALL THOSE GAMES YOU'VE PLAYED HERE... ALL THOSE MEMORIES.

I KNOW... DEMOLITION STARTS TOMORROW. PART OF ME, THE OLD FOOTBALL PART, IS GRIEVING...

...BUT MY NEW FOOTBALL SELF KNOWS THE NEW STADIUM COMPLEX IS NECESSARY, EVEN IF WE NEED ALL THAT SECOND PHASE MONEY TO START BUILDING. WE HAVE TO GO WITH THIS PROJECT, WE HAVE TO SEE IT – YES, SEE IT THROUGH.

MEANWHILE, THE SQUAD WERE TRAINING – AND PETER MARSHALL WAS STILL HAVING PROBLEMS...

GET A GRIP, PEDRO! WIPE THE BUTTER OFF YOUR FINGERS AND SORT IT OUT!

THINK I'M NOT GOOD ENOUGH – IS THAT WHAT YOU'RE SAYING?

IT WAS A JOKE, YOU PLANK! BUT SEEING AS YOU'RE ASKING – YEAH, YOU'VE BEEN CHRONIC LATELY!

46

CLUB CAPTAIN STEVE WOOTEN STEPPED IN...

THAT'S BANG OUT OF ORDER, ROCKY! GOB IN GEAR, BRAIN IN NEUTRAL YET AGAIN.

HE ASKED - I PUT HIM STRAIGHT! SOMETHING ANY SKIPPER WORTH THE ARMBAND SHOULD DO! BUT NO...

...YOU USE IT TO HAVE ANOTHER POP AT ME WHEN —

ENOUGH!

NOW, TEDDIES BACK IN PRAMS, AND LET'S GET TO WORK!

SITUATION DEFUSED, ROY SPENT THE MORNING BOOSTING HIS YOUNG 'KEEPER'S CONFIDENCE...

NOW, THERE'S A FEW THINGS I WANT YOU TO THINK ABOUT...

YOU WOULDN'T BE AT ROVERS IF YOU COULDN'T PLAY, SO FORGET ANYTHING MY SON SAID. HE COULD NO MORE KEEP GOAL THAN KEEP HIS MOUTH SHUT!

AND BEFORE THE GAME, IN THE DRESSING ROOM, ROY WAS STILL PREPARING THE PLAYER...

WHAT'S GOING ON OVER THERE, ROCKS?

RECKON MY OLD MAN'S TELLIN' MARSHALL IF HE COSTS US THIS GAME HE'LL LOCK HIM INSIDE MEL PARK WHEN THE BULLDOZERS MOVE IN!

ONE PLAYER ESPECIALLY WAS UP FOR IT...

PLAYING RAPID ALKMAR OF HOLLAND, ROVERS STARTED WELL...

GOOD EARLY PRESSURE, ROVERS! COME ON - LAST EVER GAME AT MEL PARK, WE'VE GOT TO WIN THIS!

BRILLIANT, ROCKY! LEFT TWO ON THE DECK!

47

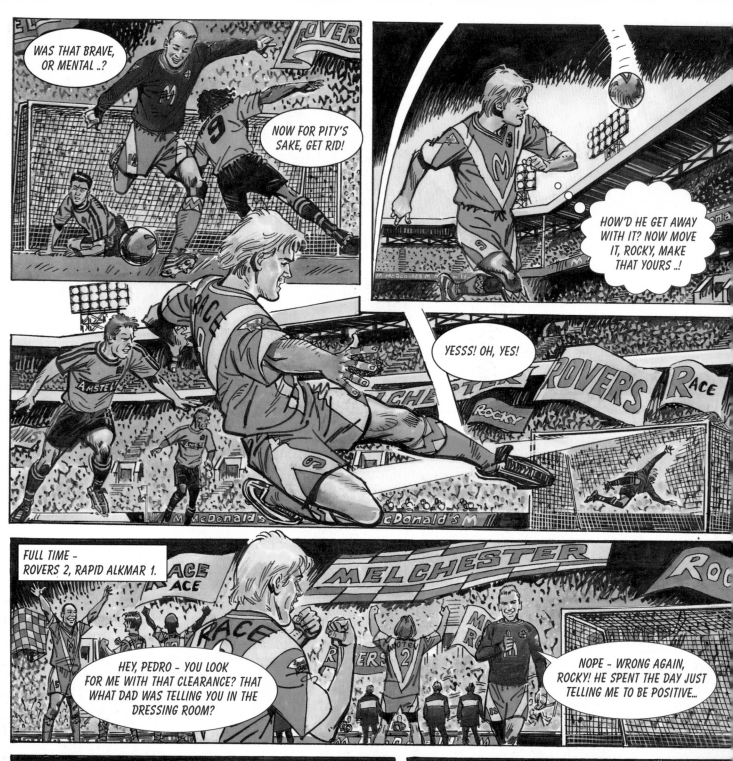

ROCKY RACE

THE NEW ROY OF THE ROVERS

While his father's influence on Melchester Rovers is still enormous, the member of the Race family who provides the moments of magic on the pitch today is Roy's son Rocky.

ROY 'Rocky' Race is most definitely not a chip off the old block. While he might have the blond hair and striking good looks, the physical similarities between father and son end there.

For some reason, Roy junior possesses none of the muscular presence Roy senior brought to the field of play. To put it bluntly, Rocky is from the stunted school of soccer.

Officially, he stands 1.725 metres short. Quite a few at Rovers, however, reckon he pulled a fast one to get himself registered that tall in the first place. Curiously, every time the club doctor produces a tape measure during pre-season, Rocky is strangely always absent.

But as we've seen with Michael Owen and Joe Cole, being almost short enough to win a cap for Lilliput is no bar to footballing excellence. The bottom line is that Rocky can play – and he can play just about anywhere.

Lacking the necessary centimetres to be a typical centre-forward, Rovers' current number nine tends to operate just behind the main striker – although he has also played in a more orthodox midfield position, and out wide. His sprinter's speed is a great asset, but it's his ball control and dribbling skills that really grab the onlooker's attention.

The simple truth of it is that Rocky is superb on the ball.

Yet it is not physique alone that marks the lad as different from his dad. The son has inherited none of the father's self-control. Being blunt again, Rocky is a hot-head. He's a fiery, competitive character who on occasions becomes a red mist merchant. This tendency of reacting before thinking has brought numerous suspensions already during his short career. Efforts have been made to curb the defect, but to date, nothing has lasted. Rocky by name, and rocky by nature it, seems.

This failing is enough for many experts and commentators to conclude that the former star of the Rovers has a distinct edge over the current one. Many, but not all, however …

One in particular is adamant that the better player of the pair is Roy of the Rovers mark two. And if anyone should know, this expert should – for his name is none other than Roy Race!

MATCH OF THE DAY's debut on our TV screens came on 22nd August 1964. A number of players born in that same season have made an impressive mark on the game. Some are still very much involved at the top level, while one looks set to tackle Hollywood. They are ...**THE MATCH OF THE DAY GENERATION**

Name: **GIANLUCA VIALLI**

Born: 9 / 7 / 64

Previous Clubs:
CREMONESE, SAMPDORIA, JUVENTUS

Currently: CHELSEA MANAGER

IF you're going to sign somebody on a free transfer, why not make it one of the finest strikers to grace the game? That's what Chelsea did, snapping up 'Luca for no Lira at all in 1996, right after he'd lifted the European Cup in his final game for Juventus. And hey, may as well make him player-manager 18 months or so later and watch the trophies start rolling in too, which is what Chelsea did again. Sadly, for those who enjoyed watching a master craftsman at work, management takes up all Vialli's time these days. His boots remain on the hanger – unlike that array of colourful ties and jumpers he wears for the post-match interviews.

Name: **GARY McALLISTER**

Born: 25 / 12 / 64

Previous Clubs:
MOTHERWELL, LEICESTER CITY, LEEDS UNITED, COVENTRY CITY

Currently: LIVERPOOL MIDFIELD LYNCHPIN

LAST season was Gary's 19th in the professional game, and in terms of personal form it was one of his best. Curiously, he might have his detractors in the Tartan Army to thank for that, because when sections of the Scottish crowd started to boo him during one or two internationals, Gary promptly packed in playing for his country. After winning 58 caps, he jettisoned all the travel and upheaval associated with international football, and a by-product has been some wonderful performances at club level. In the summer Gary joined Liverpool to add maturity to a growing squad.

Name: **VINNIE JONES**

Born: 5 / 1 / 65

Previous Clubs:
WIMBLEDON, LEEDS UNITED SHEFFIELD UNITED, CHELSEA, WIMBLEDON (2nd spell), QPR

Currently:
CELEBRITY CITY SQUAD MEMBER

MANY adjectives spring to mind when trying to sum up Vincent Jones. Mild, gentle, placid and quiet are not amongst them. He had worked as a building site hod carrier, and was playing for non-League Wealdstone, when Wimbledon brought him into the professional game. Within two seasons, he'd won an FA Cup Winner's medal. A midfield 'minder', intimidating tackler, and launcher of long throws - though not quite in the Challinor class in terms of distance – the Vinster went on to collect nine caps for Wales, numerous

The MOTD Generation

Lock, Stock and Two Smoking Barrels,

red and yellow cards, and notoriety as a hard man both on and off the field. After a hugely successful role as a gangland debt collector in the cult film Lock, Stock and Two Smoking Barrels, this rough, tough and two smoking boots footballer promptly packed in playing to pursue a film career. From hod carrier to Hollywood in thirteen tempestuous seasons. Remarkable.

WHEN it comes to claims to fame, few in the MOTD Generation, or in any other generation for that matter, can match the hat-trick Robbie Earle has notched up. What we have here, in addition to a player sharp enough to have scored more than 150 League and Cup goals, is someone who can reasonably claim to have three sets of letters after his name. You see at Wimbledon, Robbie is not only in the Crazy Gang, he skippers them! With the Reggae Boyz of Jamaica at France 98, he scored the first ever World Cup Finals goal for the country, against Croatia. And the following summer it was announced that Robbie had made the Honours List, becoming a Member of the British Empire. So that gives us Robbie Earle, CGS, RB and MBE. *(And if we were smug know-alls we'd write QED at this point – but we're not, so we won't).*

LET'S keep this simple. If you're an essential component of a 'double' winning team, you're class. If you're an essential component of a team that does the 'double' twice, you're really class. Two further titles, another FA Cup win, a League Cup success and a Cup Winners' Cup triumph also came Manchester United's way when Gary was in the side. And save for injuries, he'd have undoubtedly played more internationals than the 22 appearances he made for England. Now enjoying his second spell holding the Middlesbrough defence together, Pally and his United centre-back partner Steve Bruce were tagged 'Daisy and Dolly' by Sir Alex Ferguson. Which just goes to show that even being a class performer is no protection against a silly nickname.

Name: ROBBIE EARLE

Born: 27 / 1 / 65

Previous Club: PORT VALE

Currently: WIMBLEDON CAPTAIN AND MIDFIELDER

Name: GARY PALLISTER

Born: 30 / 6 /65

Previous Clubs: MIDDLESBROUGH, DARLINGTON (on loan), MANCHESTER UNITED

Currently: MIDDLESBROUGH'S DEFENSIVE ANCHOR

Name: TONY COTTEE

Born: 11 / 7 / 65

Previous Clubs: WEST HAM, EVERTON, WEST HAM (2nd spell), SELANGOR, BIRMINGHAM (on loan)

Currently: LEICESTER CITY GOAL POACHER

BEING on the diminutive side, we're sneaking Tony Cottee in during extra time. That's appropriate because, having been rescued from football in the Far East by Martin O'Neill, it's in this extra time of his career that TC finally became a Wembley winner at last season's Worthington Cup Final. He was the teenage scoring sensation of his day, voted PFA Young Player of the Year in 1986. A natural goalscorer, he became one of the most sought-after finishers in football. By the time he was a full England international, a big money move took him to Everton. But though that goalscorer's magic touch never left him, medals and trophies stayed out of reach. A move back to West Ham in 1994 was followed by a drift abroad. His career seemed destined for full time obscurity in Malaysia – but then along came Leicester, and that priceless extra time with a top team in the Premiership.

Other Members of the MOTD Generation Include:

Kevin BALL/ Steve BULL/Steve WALSH/
Ken MONKOU/Guy WHITTINGHAM/
Colin CALDERWOOD

IF YOU'RE GOOD ENOUGH, YOU'RE YOUNG ENOUGH!

PLAYERS OLDER THAN MOTD WHO APPEARED IN THE PREMIERSHIP LAST SEASON

PLAYER	BIRTH DATE	CLUB
Steve BOULD	16 / 11 / 62	Sunderland
Alec CHAMBERLAIN	20 / 6 / 64	Watford
Lee DIXON	17 / 3 / 64	Arsenal
John DREYER	11 / 6 / 63	Bradford
Richard GOUGH	5 / 4 / 62	Everton
Mark HUGHES	1 / 11 / 63	Everton
Stuart McCALL	10 / 6 / 64	Bradford
Stuart PEARCE	24 / 4 / 62	West Ham
Dean SAUNDERS	21 / 6 / 64	Bradford
David SEAMAN	19 / 9 / 63	Arsenal
Neville SOUTHALL	16 / 9 / 58	Bradford
Andy TOWNSEND	23 / 7 / 63	Middlesbrough
Raimond VAN DER GOUW	24 / 3 / 63	Manchester United
Dave WATSON	20 / 11 / 61	Everton
Nigel WINTERBURN	11 / 12 / 63	Arsenal

Who am I?

With a display like this at home, it's clear that this player is a very proud Scottish international. So it might surprise you to learn that he was born in Sutton, near London, in 1970.

Yet even though his roots are from south of the border, he has made sure he knows the words to *Flower of Scotland*. A call-up to the Scottish squad came when he revealed he had a Scottish Grandfather in a magazine article. He made his international debut in 1997.

He clearly has a fondness for Friends. However, in the position that he plays, if you make any mistakes, you have few of them! He also features in the video footage of one of David Beckham's finest moments, when the United player famously scored from inside his own half a few seasons ago.

Players in this star's position are often referred to as crazy, and having been a fully paid-up member of the Crazy Gang for years, the adjective is one that fits him like a glove.

His home ground for many seasons, pictured here, has really been a home from home in many ways. But during the summer, after 18 years at the club he joined as a 12-year-old, he moved to a North London side.

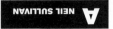

A NEIL SULLIVAN

Waving Goodbye

THE F.A. CUP SPONSORED BY AXA
WINNERS 2000

Our main pictures show Chelsea celebrating their win in May in the last ever Cup Final at the original Wembley Stadium. Roberto Di Matteo was their goal hero, as he had been for the Blues in another Final at the old Stadium. It was a place that was always a home for heroes. And down the years, there were countless other players who enjoyed great glory there.

Mark Hughes has collected four FA Cup winner's medals in his career to date; Ian Rush grabbed five goals in several FA Cup Finals; our own Trevor Brooking nodded West Ham, then of the Second Division, to an underdog triumph over Arsenal; Sunderland's goalscorer, Ian Porterfield, and goalkeeper, Jim Montgomery, were giants in their astounding 1973 win over the all-powerful Leeds' side; the two Stans –

Mortensen with his hat-trick and Matthews with his creative play – tore Bolton to shreds in Blackpool's 4-3 win in 1953.

More Wembley heroes emerged in other great competitions, like Sir Matt Busby's 1968 Manchester United side, which became the first from England to win the European Cup. And, of course, there's no forgetting Sir Alf Ramsey, his men, and English football's finest moment in 1966, when Bobby Moore lifted the World Cup.

However, not all Wembley heroes have been football ones. Bob Geldof's Live Aid concert in 1985 raised funds for the starving of Africa – saving millions of lives. And lives were undoubtedly saved at the very first Cup Final at Wembley in 1923 by PC George Scorey and his famous white police horse,

Billy. Then, an estimated 200,000 people squeezed into the stadium for the West Ham v Bolton Final, but they were marshalled superbly by the single horse and rider.

That story is part of football folklore, as are elements of the stadium itself. Wembley Way ... The Twin Towers ... Tied ribbons on the trophy ... Climbing the steps to the Royal Box ... Up for the Cup ..! Just add 'jumpers for goal-posts' and you've got a speech by Ron Manager.

To Wembley

Big Wembley Occasions ...

Below – Liverpool celebrate winning the European Cup in 1978.

Far Right – an aerial shot of the first-ever Wembley Cup Final, played in 1923 between Bolton and West Ham. Over 200,000 fans crammed into the newly-constructed Stadium.

Far right (2nd pic) – England win the 1966 World Cup and Bobby Moore and the lads are the toast of the nation.

Which, when you think about it, tells you why the old place is being pulled down. Let's be honest – the structure had become something of a soccer cliché itself. That said, there's no denying that Wembley was the setting for the very finest football memories the nation has. So one final cliché is also true of the place – in all the years of service that Wembley has given the game, surely it's football that's been the winner there.

Over the past 30 years MOTD has witnessed some remarkable changes to 'the beautiful game'. So what do the next three decades have to offer ..? We take a not-very-serious look at soccer's future in ...

21ST CENTURY FOOTBALL

2001 - TIGANA does the trick, and Fulham return to the top flight of English football for the first time since the 1967-68 season. Unlikely as it sounds, Jimmy Hill is rendered speechless. Meanwhile, Tony Ford, the first outfield player to clock up 1,000 League appearances, is still playing.

2002 - It looks for a time as if Pele might have been only a couple of years out with his famous prediction that a team from Africa would win the World Cup before the 21st century when Nigeria sensationally reach the tournament Final played in Japan. However, it is the brilliant Spaniards, putting decades and decades of World Cup underachievement behind them, who lift the trophy after a magnificent 3-1 victory.

2003 - Referees in England turn professional. They also turn to technology for help in tricky goal-line decisions with the insertion of a special sensor inside footballs which indicates whether or not the ball has crossed the line between the posts. A new set of clichés is born: "That sensor is a homer!", "The sensor bottled it!" "We'll get nothing from that sensor today!"

2004 - In a variation on squad rotation, and in a bid to end their years of domestic dominance coupled with European failure, Rangers introduce Manager rotation. They employ one boss to wear the Ibrox sheepskin for Scottish Premier League matches, and use a second 'gaffer' to guide them through European games. Years of domestic dominance coupled with European failure are indeed brought to an end – Celtic win the Scottish title.

2005 - The number of front-line officials for Premiership games grows to five when instant TV replays are introduced for controversial incidents. The new member of the team, the 'video official', adjudicates by studying TV monitors. When a borderline decision goes against him, one hot-headed Italian player pushes over a TV monitor and is banned for 12 matches.

2006 - There is an eerily familiar World Cup tournament in Germany. Scotland fail to make it past the first phase, being eliminated on goal difference. England, managed by Bryan Robson,

lose a semi-final penalty shoot-out to Germany. Brazil triumph overall, following a Ronaldo hat-trick in the Final itself. The gap-toothed one, having finally proved himself the world's greatest player, promptly retires from the game. Not so Tony Ford, who has now played more than 1,200 games.

2007 - Manchester United withdraw from all domestic Cup competitions, citing fixture congestion and fear of player injury, and concentrate solely on the Premiership and the ever-expanding Champions League.

2008 - Sponsorship in football continues to spread. Yellow Pages agree a deal with the FA to sponsor referees' yellow cards.

2009 - David Beckham returns from a three-year spell with AC Milan in Italy and buys Scarborough FC as a present for wife Victoria. A rumour quickly spreads that he really meant to buy Peterborough because of that club's coincidental 'Posh' nickname, but he actually got confused. Nevertheless, Victoria wastes no time in installing her hubby as player-manager and signing up her son for the club's youth academy.

2010 - When England, Northern Ireland, Scotland and Wales, together with the Republic of Ireland, fail to make the World Cup Finals in Brazil, domestic support switches to France, under new manager David Ginola.

2011 - Football boot technology reaches new levels with telescopic studs. They automatically adjust in length according to pitch conditions, seemingly ending all those pre-match debates about whether a short or long stud is needed. After only a handful of games, however, they are banned when a player raises his boot in a challenge and his studs telescope through an opponent's shinguard.

2012 - Manchester United withdraw from domestic competition altogether, citing fixture congestion in a still ever-expanding Champions League.

2013 - Scarborough win the Premiership title.

2014 - Of the home nations only Wales fails to qualify for the Australian World Cup. To no-one's surprise, England, Scotland and N. Ireland are drawn with the Republic of Ireland in the same group. The Keane Republic – managed by Roy, captained by Robbie – are runners-up behind an Alan Shearer coached England, and they pip Scotland, as always, on goal difference. England and the Republic crash out at the quarter-final stage, while the home nation triumphs thanks to a wonder goal from Harry Kewell. It's officially the 124th wonder goal of his career.

2015 - Wales slide further down FIFA's world rankings. A former Welsh wizard of the dribble fears that "at this rate, by 2020 we'll be below San Marino."

2016 - Scarborough beat Manchester United in the first ever all-English Champions League Final. One B. Beckham makes his debut as a sub in the Final, and scores the winner.

2017 - Wales slip below San Marino in FIFA's world rankings. "Told you," says a former Welsh wizard of the dribble.

2018 - Scotland are the only qualifiers from these parts to make the World Cup Finals in China. Coached by Darren Ferguson (who takes along his dad, Sir Alex, to show him how to throw tea cups and keep time) they show a shocking disregard for history and qualify for the second phase, only to be knocked out straight away by surprise package San Marino.

2019 - Sky TV ups the technology content of football another notch by introducing the blade-of-grass cam – a micro-miniature camera positioned on one tip of a piece of turf behind the goal-line. Early outings for the experiment are encouraging, but an overzealous groundsman at Arsenal cuts the grass too short before a live game, and the camera is lost in the cuttings.

21st Century Football

2020 - Michael Owen dons the nation's sheep-skin coat to take charge of England. He makes Brooklyn Beckham his captain.

2021 - After tireless decades of campaigning by 84-year-old Sir Bobby Charlton, FIFA at last agrees to award the 2026 World Cup to England .

2022 - Following global warming, and FIFA's drive to take football to every continent of the globe, Antarctica stages the World Cup. Owen's England perform creditably but the words 'semi-final', 'Germany' and 'penalties' once again precede another familiar word, 'elimination'.

2023 - Tests with robot officials lead to a strike by their flesh and blood counterparts, who feel their careers and livelihoods are threatened. Minus match officials, football is stopped for weeks until administrators cave in and agree to give robo refs a permanent red card.

2024 - Suddenly aware of their power, referees demand and receive vastly improved salaries. Agents move in to represent the top officials in Europe. Matching players and their boot deals, several refs sign whistle deals while some assistants obtain lucrative flag contracts.

2025 - Tigana Haynes, born on the day Fulham won promotion to the Premiership in 2001 and named after the then manager, signs a new contract with the club which makes him the country's first £1,000,000-a-week player.

2026 - With the World Cup Finals back in England, aging comedians Baddiel and Skinner come out of retirement to re-release "Football's Coming Home". It contains slightly modified lyrics such as "Sixty years of hurt, never stopped me dreaming". This time it works, and England, under the astute managership of Joe Cole, are crowned World Champions again.

2027 - ITV finally updates its logo for The Big Match.

2028 - Tony Ford retires.

2029 - A surprising report reveals that the overwhelming majority of Manchester United supporters actually live in Southern Europe.

2030 - A clone of Tony Ford makes his League debut in the Premiership.

*EURO 2000 had everything. Game after game of high-class football in the Low Countries, with France's team of all-talents taking home the trophy. In short it was... **MAGNIFIQUE!***

It doesn't get much better than that! The finest international tournament for 30 years was simply great stuff – some truly great games, starring some great players, who produced some great moments of skill that will live long in the memory.

The flair, inventiveness and finishing of the likes of Zidane, Figo, Totti, Henry, and Kluivert, to name just a few, at times pushed the football towards fantasy levels. So many games produced open, attacking play. So many sides went into matches looking to win them. So few coaches employed stifling tactics to avoid defeat. Even England, netting five times in three games, carried an impressive goal threat.

Nuno Gomes

Skills and touch on the ball – honed in the warmer southern European nations like Portugal, Spain, Italy and Yugoslavia, and protected by the tougher line taken by officials to tackling from behind – generally outshone and outclassed the organisation and work-rate of players from the cooler north, such as the Scandinavian countries, Germany and England. France, it could be argued, had the perfect blend, with a sizeable number of their squad hailing from the country's more equatorial former colonies.

If that is one factor in France's current domination of world football, there are many others. Zinedine Zidane, for instance. If you've got the best player in the world performing at his best, you're in with a chance. The team is pep-

A. Shearer
S. McManaman

pered with other world-class performers too, and as a unit it has no weaknesses. Above all, perhaps, is the strength of character the World Champions have – and which all great teams possess – which allows them to dismiss the prospect of defeat no matter how inevitable it seems. A late, late equaliser, with a winner to follow? Like watching Manchester United, wasn't it?

Which brings us to England. No, it wasn't good. Yet, just perhaps, amid the scathing criticism and the scramble to dish out blame which followed that early exit, maybe the one or two positives that were in evidence have been overlooked.

As mentioned already, England did threaten going forward – the second against Portugal, for instance, in terms of build-up and finish, was a little gem of a goal. David Beckham and Paul Scholes both performed well, and while many have moaned that only those two could be called world-class, that's two more world-class players than many other nations have got. Plus, in Michael Owen – who got better with each game – and Steven Gerrard, England had two of the youngest players on view, and they will improve. And finally, if nothing else, everyone – from manager and players all the way down to the fans – seemed at last to grasp the golden rule of international football, that passing the ball poorly and giving it away cheaply, as England did, spells doom.

If recognising a problem is the biggest obstacle to curing it, England's dismal

showing in EURO 2000 might one day be seen as a blessing in disguise.

F. Barthez, France

MOTD Annual's TEAM OF THE TOURNAMENT

Francesco TOLDO, Italy

Lilian THURAM, France

Alessandro NESTA, Italy

Marcel DESAILLY, France

Paolo MALDINI, Italy

David BECKHAM, England

Edgar DAVIDS, Holland

Zinedine ZIDANE, France

Luis FIGO, Portugal

Patrick KLUIVERT, Holland

Thierry HENRY, France

Francesco TOLDO, Italy

A late stand-in for Buffon in the Italian goal, and a giant at 6ft 5ins, Toldo produced some immense performances, not least in thwarting Holland's penalty takers in the semi-final.

Alessandro NESTA, Italy

A central defender in the classical tradition of his countrymen, he was at the heart of every Italian rearguard action throughout EURO 2000. The tournament's top defender.

Lilian THURAM, France

Following a faultless World Cup two years ago, Thuram shone once again at right-back. The scary thing is he's said to be even better at the centre of the back line, where he's expected to take over soon from Laurent Blanc.

Paolo MALDINI, Italy

Supposedly slipping past his very best, Maldini – only two caps away from eclipsing Dino Zoff's record number of appearances for Italy – was still a vital performer in that stubborn defence, either at left full-back or wing-back.

Marcel DESAILLY, France

Powerful and athletic, yet composed and controlled with it, the imperious Chelsea centre-back oozed class in almost every aspect of his play.

David BECKHAM, England

One of the very few players from this country who enhanced his reputation at EURO 2000. That fantastic right foot of his set up three of the five goals England scored.

Edgar DAVIDS, Holland

The guy in the goggles pumped so much energy, effort, enthusiasm – and no little skill – into the Dutch midfield. A really dynamic operator in the middle of the park.

Euro 2000

Zinedine ZIDANE, France

The French playmaker whose form and touch was at times breathtaking. The outstanding member of an outstanding team, and currently rated the world's best player.

Patrick KLUIVERT, Holland

The joint-top scorer at EURO 2000 who looked to be back to his sharp and lethal best in front of goal. The only Dutchman to convert a penalty in that fateful semi-final failure.

Thierry HENRY, France

Gazelle-like striker with tremendous speed, he troubled every opposition back line that he faced. An assured, composed finisher and a constant source of danger.

N. Gomes,

Luis FIGO, Portugal

Exceptionally talented and versatile danger-man who popped up all over the place for Portugal, and who is able to weave his magic from any position across the middle of the pitch, or even up front.